On The Montana Homestead

10 Years of Unforgettable Episodes, 1913–1924

Rev. Abraham A. Becker

On The Montana Homestead © copyright 2023 by Abraham A. Becker. All rights reserved. No part of this book may be reproduced in any form whatsoever, by photography or xerography or by any other means, by broadcast or transmission, by translation into any kind of language, nor by recording electronically or otherwise, without permission in writing from the author, except by a reviewer, who may quote brief passages in critical articles or reviews.

All scriptures taken from the Holy Bible, are from the New International Version®, NIV®. Copyright © 1973, 1978, 1984, 2011 by Biblica, Inc.™ Used by permission of Zondervan. All rights reserved worldwide.

Hardcover ISBN: 979-8-218-16383-9
eBook ISBN: 979-8-218-16384-6

Book cover and interior design by Jess LaGreca, Mayfly Design

Library of Congress Catalog Number: 2023903544
First Printing: 2023
Printed in United States of America

Contents

FOREWORD: Stephen B. Becker v
INTRODUCTION: Revisiting Childhood Days in Montana 1

Becker Montana Homestead: Abraham A Becker 3
Episodes 9
Transition Back to South Dakota 57
Preparing to Move 61
Mother's Closing Role 67
Father's Closing Role 77
Reflecting Back 83

AFTERWORD: Stephen B. Becker 85

Foreword

My father, Abraham A. Becker, captured his childhood memories in this book, giving us a glimpse of daily life in the early 1900s of homesteaders in Montana.

As a young man, my grandfather, Abraham B. Becker, must have desired the best for his family. His father, Heinrich Benjamin Becker, had homesteaded in South Dakota, and Abraham must have longed to do the same for his family. It is helpful to understand the Mennonite heritage and life experiences of his father to better understand the daring move Abraham made to relocate his family to Montana.

The teachings of the Mennonites, a group of Christian Anabaptist denominations named after Menno Simons (1496–1561), were founded on the mission and ministry of Jesus Christ, which they held to with great conviction despite persecution. Over the years, Mennonites have become known as one of the historic peace churches given their commitment to nonviolence.

Most of our low German ancestors were Anabaptists before moving from Germany to Holland. Anabaptists are Christians of the Radical Reformation of the Catholic Church led by Martin Luther and others. Anabaptists rejected church tradition such as wearing wedding rings, taking oaths, and participating in state government. They adhered to a literal interpretation of the Sermon on the Mount and Believer's baptism, in which their name, Anabaptist, is derived. A splinter group of Anabaptists that did not believe in military service were first called

Mennists and later called Mennonites, after their famous leader Menno Simons, a former Roman Catholic priest. Not being tolerated in Holland, our Dutch forebears were pressured into leaving, starting in the mid-1550s.

The Prussian nobility of the Vistula River Valley heard of the Mennonites and their skills and abilities in the art of reclaiming swamplands by means of dikes and canals. Sometime around 1550, a large number of Dutch Mennonites moved to the lowland deltas of the Vistula River of Western Elbing, and Przechowka areas.

They soon built thriving villages from the former flooded swamps, creating tillable soil of the once-unusable land. They introduced purebred lines of livestock and used their skills to make cheese and butter, which had a ready market in the nearby towns.

By 1772, Frederick the Great had united East and West Prussia and given the Mennonites guarantees that Mennonites would not have to serve in the military. Things looked very bright. Mennonites had been driven from place to place by persecution, so the privileges of religious freedom, their own schools, self-government, and especially military exemption was very enticing to them. Unfortunately that did not last long, and harassment resumed. They started once again looking at locations to move to in their efforts to protect their religious freedom.

Russian Empress Catherine II invited the Mennonites to settle in southern Russia in an area now known as Ukraine, offering them a 100-year exemption from military service. They settled into areas about 200 miles west of Kiev, establishing fifty villages along the Molostschna and Volga rivers, where they greatly prospered. Others decided it would be better to be back under Polish rule and moved into regions close to Ostrog where they founded the village circuit of Karolswalde, taking their German and Low Dutch language.

Abraham B. and Helena Becker's ancestors settled in the village of Antonovka in Volhynia, Russia. Bronnyky, Rivnens'ka oblast Ukraine is very close to the old village of Antonovka.

The birthplace of Heinrich Benjamin Becker was approximately 200 miles west of Kyiv.

After Catherine II died, the new ruler wanted to terminate the special privileges of the Mennonites. Compulsory military service followed with a new decree stating that in 1889 any remaining Mennonites would lose their passports and all exemptions.

Once again Mennonites decided to investigate a new location that would allow religious freedom. A delegation of twelve men was chosen and sent to America to look things over and examine colonization possibilities there. They looked at the middle states and returned to share the opportunity to own land through a homestead provision in America and the freedom to worship unhampered by government. They did not obtain the promise of military exemption but were quite assured that wars were not in the realm of possibility in this country, so they were willing to take a chance on that. Most Mennonites decided to leave for America.

Divine guidance was with them for they could not possibly have known that, in a few generations, the area they were leaving would be visited by the severe turmoil of World War I followed by the tragic Bolshevik Revolution, and then again by World War II. A terrible fate befell those who remained in Russia and Poland as families were separated and sent to far-off Siberia and others were sent to slave labor camps where they died slow deaths.

The fortunate ones who decided to leave for America suffered loss as they left. Since they did not own the land they lived on in Russia; all they could do was sell their assets in a desperate market to potential buyers who knew they were leaving. Some could sell nothing and had to abandon their property. Mennonites in America arranged for loans and negotiated reduced rates with ship lines and railroads to help German Mennonites in Russia to escape.

Heinrich Benjamin Becker, his wife Susanna, and their four children left Karlswalde, Russia, on November 23, 1874, with his parents, Jacob B. and Elizabeth J. (Koehn) Becker. They arrived in Philadelphia on January 8, 1875. Heinrich Benjamin Becker and his family remained in Pennsylvania with Mennonites, then in the spring they went by rail to Yankton, South Dakota. They ventured north of Yankton without the benefit of road or guide. There they found a Hutterite colony that had settled in the summer of 1874 on the east side of Silver Lake.

Hutterites are a communal branch of Anabaptists who, like Amish and Mennonites, trace their roots to the Radical Reformation of the sixteenth century. Since the death of their founder Jakob Hutter in 1536, the beliefs of the Hutterites, especially living in a community of goods and absolute pacifism, resulted in hundreds of years of odyssey through many countries. Nearly extinct by the eighteenth and nineteenth century, the Hutterites found a new home in North America. Over 125 years their population grew from 400 to around 50,000.

The Hutterite colony consisted of four sod houses, each with two rooms approximately sixteen-by-sixteen feet, with a ten-foot alley between the rooms. The Beckers purchased one of the sod homes and lived in it the summer of 1875, while building a sod house to call their own.

Heinrich Benjamin Becker's wife Susanna passed away September 8, 1975, leaving him a widower with four young sons. In March of 1876 Heinrich married Susanna Koehn. She must have been a special young woman at the age of sixteen to take on the responsibility of his four sons, ages four to eight. She would eventually have eleven children. Abraham B. Becker was her fifth child, born May 13, 1884.

Abraham grew to manhood on the prairie of South Dakota and married Helena B. Buller on September 21, 1908. Helena's family had migrated from the same village in Russia with hundreds of other German Mennonites who all moved at the same time. As their family grew, Abraham became eager to homestead a place for himself, just like his father had done in South Dakota. Unfortunately, there was no longer any land available to homestead in South Dakota in the early 1900s, and his homestead options were mostly limited to Montana, unless he was willing to leave the country and move to Canada. He must have seen marketing pieces printed by the Great Northern Railroad, promoting Montana as a perfect place to homestead. He decided to try his luck there. My father, Abraham A. Becker, was the youngest of the three children, and not yet one year old.

The original Homestead Act was signed by Abraham Lincoln on May 20, 1862, and later updated. The Act required that an applicant be twenty-one years old, live on the homestead for five years, and improve the property. In exchange, he or she would receive title to the land. Initially the Act limited the size of land to 160 acres. It was amended to allow up to 320 acres of government land with only a ten-dollar filing fee. Abraham B. Becker elected to take the full 320 acres available at the time he filed. The parcel adjoining Abraham B. Becker's was filed by his sister, Helena Boldt, using her maiden name, Helena B. Becker. Many Beckers homesteaded; however it does not appear any of the other Beckers' noted were from South Dakota.

The homestead era in Montana lasted for more than seventy years; however most of homesteading took place during a ten-year period between 1908 and 1918. Most of these families were lured by a slick advertising campaign paid for by railroad magnate James J. Hill, who controlled the Great Northern, the Burlington, and the Northern Pacific railroads. Hill knew that customers for his railroads were hard to find in sparsely populated Montana. Hill realized that with the help of the Homestead Act, he could convert the empty plains of Montana into a potential gold mine for his railroad empire. All he had to do was convince potential farmers that the dry plains of Montana were rich farmland.

By 1908 Jim Hill's Great Northern Railroad campaign to bring thousands of small farmers into Montana was in full swing, with thousands of color brochures distributed throughout the United States and European countries extolling the virtues of the Great Plains. Mr. Hill ran railway exhibit cars in the Midwest, and it is likely that Abraham saw one of these exhibits. Hill also hired an agricultural expert, Professor Thomas Shaw, who described eastern Montana as a "farmer's paradise." By 1910, Shaw was operating forty-five experimental farms in Montana, and the favorable results of his experiments were widely publicized. The same year the Abraham B. Becker family moved to Montana, 1913, was a peak year for homesteading

Along with promoting the promise of free land in an agricultural paradise, Hill announced cut-rate fares on his railroad to entice farmers to move to the state. For as little as $22.50, a homesteader could rent a freight car to bring his family and all their belongings from Saint Paul to eastern Montana. The population of Montana grew from 376,053 in 1910 to 584,889 in 1920, most of it in the northeastern counties. This attests to the success of Hill's marketing and promotions. More than thirty million acres of public land in Montana was granted to private owners under the Homestead Act. These farmers bought wagons, machinery, building materials, and fencing that were all shipped at normal freight rates. In 1924, two freight cars returning the Beckers to South Dakota cost over $700. Mr. Hill's marketing genius paid off handsomely for his railroad.

How Abraham and Helena settled on the area north of Chinook is not known. Chinook is the county seat of Blaine County. The county is very large, 4,289 square miles, more than twice the size of the state of Rhode Island. Northern Blaine County was cattle and sheep country in 1910 prior to the homesteading rush. The Battle of Bear Paws, fought 15 miles south of Chinook, was the last *battle* of the Nez Perce Flight of 1877. The Nez Perce were a band of 800 men women and children fleeing from the U.S. Army.

Fort Belcamp Reservation covers a considerable part of Blaine County; Harlem was the headquarters for Indiana affairs and many Indians lived there. Tom O'Hanlon, a leading merchant in Chinook, was part Indian. I suspect that my grandparents' and my parents' affection for Native Americans came from being around them growing up in Montana. One of my favorite memories of Mom and Dad was when at age eighty, they volunteered to be leaders in a Vacation Bible School for

My mother, Elizabeth Becker, teaching Native children

Native American children in the summer of 1993. My parents lived in a tent for the week in the hot South Dakota summer.

Montana land is not nearly as rich as the farmland of South Dakota that grandfather Abraham was used to. Montana land varies significantly in richness and climate, as it is a large state. The area around Chinook is not the best in Montana, and surprisingly the area north of Chinook is not as good as the area south of Chinook. To put this in perspective, a farmer in Kansas needs only one acre of pasture per head of cattle vs. forty-five acres in the area north of Chinook where Abraham homesteaded.

My grandfather had no way to know just how poor the land in Montana was when he made the decision to move his family from South Dakota. The entire homestead venture was doomed for failure before it ever began. To provide a more current perspective: the 2023 owner, Joey Malsam, of the Montana land that Abraham homesteaded, farms and ranches 33,000 thousand acres with his two sons. Joey's home is located about a mile North of St. Rte. 2. No one lives north of him in the thirty miles to the Canadian border or in the hundreds of thousands of acres of surrounding prairie.

The closest town to grandfather's homestead was Chinook. Raw land required building materials. With a population of 1,400, Chinook lacked the offerings of a larger city, but it was the best they had available. Chinook was 19.3 miles from the homestead land. This distance may not sound like much, but consider that everything purchased in Chinook had to be transported by horse-drawn wagon at an average speed of about three miles per hour. Trips to Chinook required spending the night and returning the next day.

Abraham B Becker moved to Montana in the fall of 1913 and filed his homestead claim, which was officially recorded five years later, on February 14, 1918. When he moved to Montana in 1913, he had three children at home all under the age of four. A large family with so many young children, under such difficult conditions, had to be a drain of precious physical and mental energy. Had Abraham's children been older, they could have been more of a help during the homestead period instead of an added burden. It is amazing that Grandmother Helena (Lena) was able to keep her sanity, moving with three little children and then giving birth to five more during the next ten years on the Montana prairie.

In the first three years after moving to Montana, it appeared as if the farmers were actually successful and prospering in spite of the small size of their farms. World War I broke out in 1914, and artificially inflated grain prices rose to unprecedented levels. Montana's high-protein, hard spring and winter wheat held top rank on the booming international markets. A period of unusually high rainfall blessed the new farmers, and the normally dry prairies produced record crops of wheat.

The Havre Weather Station reported 20.71 inches of rain in 1916, 13.6 inches falling in the growing season. Little did the homesteaders know that the next bumper crop would not be until 1927, when most of them would have given up the struggle and moved away. Amazing to me is that the Abraham B. Becker family was able to remain on the homestead for ten years in spite of all the challenges. His foresight to build a reservoir and cistern must have been a lifesaver during periods of drought.

A turbulent year came for the Montana homesteaders and for the nation as it joined World War I in 1917. An influenza epidemic started the same year and lasted through 1918. The epidemic was unparalleled in modern history, killing many homesteaders who are now buried in unusual locations scattered across the desolate Montana prairie. The spring rains failed to appear in 1917 and, by the summer of 1918, drought was widespread. The Havre weather station reported only 13.66 inches of rain in 1917, with only 3.58 inches during the growing season.

The situation worsened in 1918 with only 10.04 inches of rain for the year and only 3.18 inches during the growing season. Suddenly thousands of Montana's homesteaders were in serious trouble. Their crops burned up in the fields, and nonstop winds blew away the carefully plowed and powdered topsoil. Finally, hordes of grasshoppers arrived to complete the devastation. As the semi-arid nature of the land expressed itself, the homesteaders developed a gang spirit against Jim Hill personally. He was the villain who got them into this mess.

By the fall of 1918, the war in Europe was coming to an end, and the depression was starting. There appeared to be no end in sight. Many farmers were unable to pay their bills. By the summer of 1919, thousands had been forced from their farms. Only 8.85 inches of rain came in the entire year of 1919. The same railroads, which had brought the homesteaders into Montana, now carried them away. The banks, seed merchants, and implement dealers, all of whom had fueled the homestead boom with easy credit, declared bankruptcy in record numbers.

Scripture says that God opposes the proud, but gives grace to the humble. I believe my grandfather left Montana broken in spirit, but full of God's loving grace.

—Stephen B. Becker, son of Abraham A. Becker
and grandson of Abraham B. Becker

INTRODUCTION

Revisiting Childhood Days in Montana

I had moved away from Montana in February of 1924 and had not been back to Chinook in over sixty-five years. I had almost given up the idea of making a trip to Montana, but God's providence was clear; it was God's will that we make a trip west in the summer of 1989. Elizabeth and I would be taking a second honeymoon excursion to Montana at age seventy-six.

We arrived on Friday, August 4, 1989, and stayed at the Chinook Hotel where we quickly became friends with the owners, Ted and Margaret Simpson, and visited Bessie Slonaker who, at age ninety-seven, had a keen memory of the homestead days.

We saw sights along the Clary Coulee Trail, grazing cattle and beautiful wheat fields. I could envision my father with his Avery

Abraham B. and Helena B. (Buller) Becker marriage picture, September 21, 1908. Mother made her own wedding dress.

tractor and 4-bottom plow with big rocks on top. I could see him with his four-horse team dragging dirt up the big hill and dumping it high up on the dam. Also we climbed Butte-Hill and beheld the beauties of the Choteau Coulee Trail. Looking toward Geo Class, I remembered working two days with a team of horses, picking potatoes for four silver dollars. My mind raced with the memories. After four nights in Chinook, the second honeymoon was coming to its close as we headed back to South Dakota.

I find myself amazed to write of our ten-year Montana homesteading history and grateful for the memories God preserved for future generations. My entire soul desires to not forget those lessons learned on the prairie. It is with a prayerful attitude, that I invite divine guidance and providence that these pages may serve as a memorial to reveal God's glorious purpose in what appeared to be failure of the homestead in Montana.

Abraham A. and Elizabeth Becker, age seventy-six

Becker Montana Homestead: Abraham A. Becker

1913 HOMESTEAD

It was in the fall of 1913 that my father, Abraham B. Becker Sr., filed a Homesteading Claim for 320 acres located about 19 miles North of Chinook, Montana, and 20 miles south of Canada. During this time period, several men were venturing out to take advantage of the Homestead Act that would give title to land if the homesteader would live on it for five years and improve the property. The plan was to stake a claim and build a home in preparation of moving his family early the following spring of 1914. Father, Abraham B. Becker, built a two-story house and painted it yellow. He also improvised a small reservoir dam for water to feed cattle.

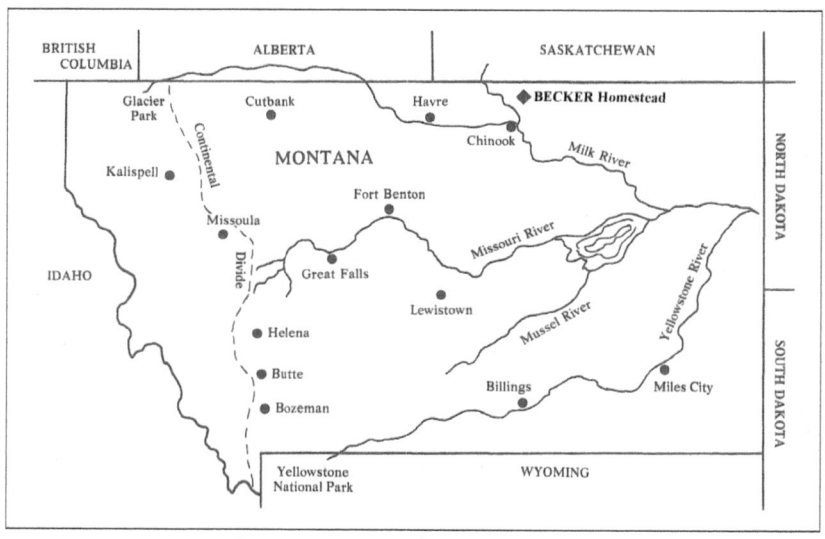

Becker Homestead

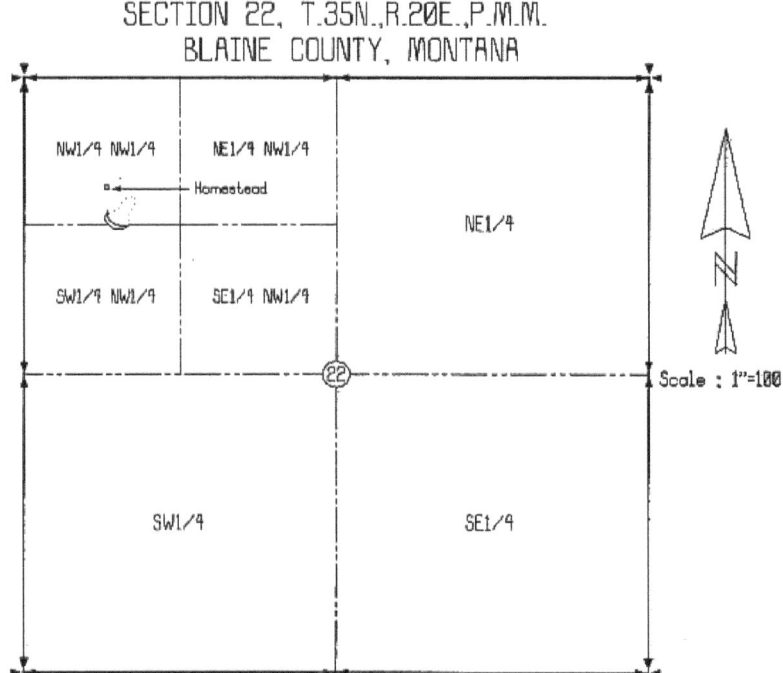

Abraham B. Becker secured both the NW ¼ and NE ¼ of section 22. The home, dam, and cistern were all located in the northwest portion of his land.

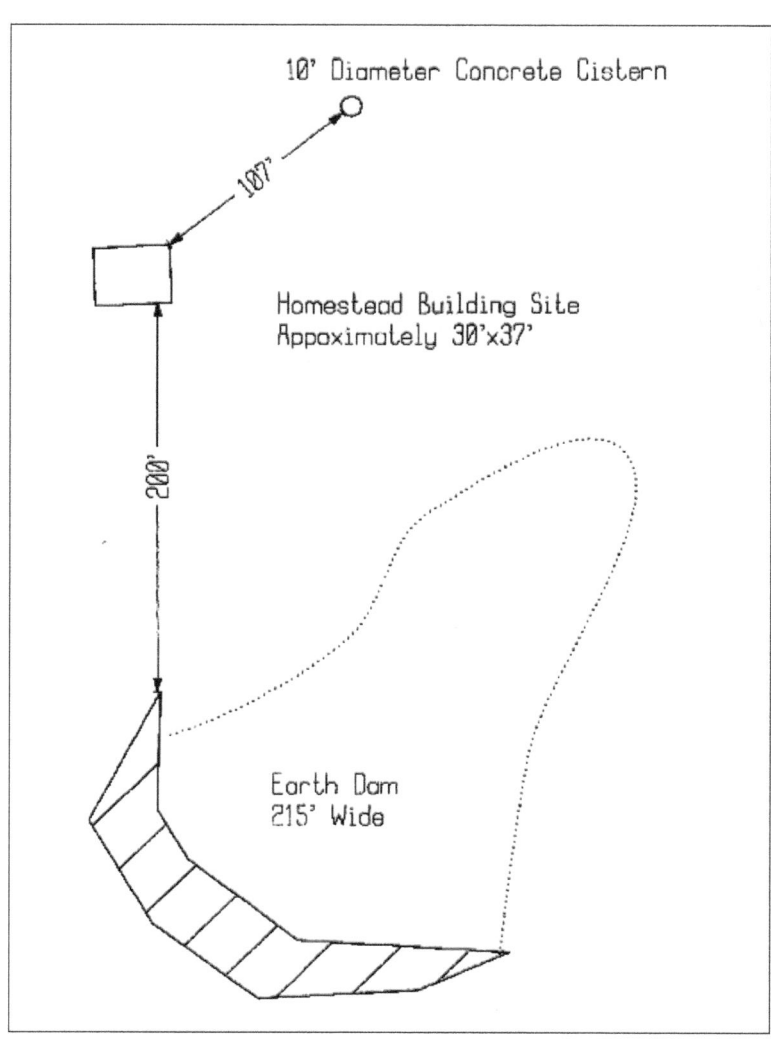

The dam was dug with mules.

2013 photo: According to the surveyor, this is the only cistern of this size and quality he knew from the time period. L to R: Stephen Becker, his son Benjamin Becker, uncle Lewis Becker, and cousin Mark Becker.

Havre 018124

4—1003-R.

The United States of America,

To all to whom these presents shall come, Greeting:

WHEREAS, a Certificate of the Register of the Land Office at **Havre, Montana,** has been deposited in the General Land Office, whereby it appears that, pursuant to the Act of Congress of May 20, 1862, "To Secure Homesteads to Actual Settlers on the Public Domain," and the acts supplemental thereto, the claim of **Abraham B. Becker** has been established and duly consummated, in conformity to law, for the **north half of Section twenty-two in Township thirty-five north of Range twenty east of the Montana Meridian, Montana, containing three hundred twenty acres,** according to the Official Plat of the Survey of the said Land, returned to the GENERAL LAND OFFICE by the Surveyor-General:

NOW KNOW YE, That there is, therefore, granted by the UNITED STATES unto the said claimant the tract of Land above described; TO HAVE AND TO HOLD the said tract of Land, with the appurtenances thereof, unto the said claimant and to the heirs and assigns of the said claimant forever; subject to any vested and accrued water rights for mining, agricultural, manufacturing, or other purposes, and rights to ditches and reservoirs used in connection with such water rights, as may be recognized and acknowledged by the local customs, laws, and decisions of courts; and there is reserved from the lands hereby granted, a right of way thereon for ditches or canals constructed by the authority of the United States.

IN TESTIMONY WHEREOF, I, **Woodrow Wilson** President of the United States of America, have caused these letters to be made Patent, and the seal of the General Land Office to be hereunto affixed.

GIVEN under my hand, at the City of Washington, the **FOURTEENTH** day of **FEBRUARY** in the year of our Lord one thousand nine hundred and **EIGHTEEN** and of the Independence of the United States the one hundred and **FORTY-SECOND.**

(SEAL)

By the President: *Woodrow Wilson*

By *M. P. LeRoy*, Secretary.

L. Q. C. Lamar, Recorder of the General Land Office.

RECORD OF PATENTS: Patent Number 616978

Land Patent #616978 for 320 acres, dated February 14, 1918 (Valentine's Day)

Episodes

FIRST WHEAT CROP
37 BU. PER ACRE

Father started farming cautiously, using only a walking plow that allowed him to watch the maturing new civilization around him as he plowed his fields. Father's first wheat crop yielded thirty-seven bushels to the acre. With the 1914 war price of four dollars per bushel for wheat, a small ankle box of wheat at the elevator yielded hundreds of dollars. The mood of the day was optimistic among the homesteaders.

The only photo left of the one-and-half-story home built during 1913–1914

In those days a helping hand became very scarce. To harvest his thirty-seven bushels per acre, Father brought home two city fellows to shock that bountiful wheat crop. These two city fellows did not know how to work on the farm and did not have a good work ethic. As soon as their boss, Mr. Becker, had passed by them with his new binder, they would stop working and sit and talk. In the mornings, while Father did all the chores, they snored and slept in. Then after a few callings, Father walked the stairs, and he found them still sleeping (in the nude). They *were* "good" at eating big meals and doing "minimal" work. Father wound up taking them back to Chinook after seeing the quality of their work.

WATER PROBLEMS

Moving to the Becker ranch required new adjustments and created some new problems. The large reservoir had not yet filled with water, and there was a little dam to the south. Father used a large water-tank wagon to transport water back and forth to the house. The sub-zero weather was about to freeze the small dam, and Father and Mother talked between themselves about the severity of the situation and decided that a temporary cistern in the porch entry would provide a short-term solution until the large cistern could be built.

COYOTES

In 1914 Mother and Father purchased a flock of chickens. Soon Father noticed that the number of chickens was dwindling. Very early one morning, Father thought that he spied dogs jumping around the chicken pen; but when he tried to chase them away, he discovered that they were coyotes. He then got busy with a shotgun.

A HORSE OF A DIFFERENT COLOR

In 1914, horses were in great demand in Montana. One of our new mare colts we found for sale was a rare Indian trotter. Some called these horses "blue horses" because of their color of hair, a rat-mouse or dark-gray. When Dick was a young colt, not yet a year old, he lay down in some new straw and slept. As he slept, he sank deeper and deeper into the straw until he was unable to rise when he tried. Practically lying on his back, he labored so strenuously that he pushed his bowels out. Father came upon the situation at the straw stack, but he was not about to give up his choice colt. He washed the bowel and shoved it all back into the young animal. Dick survived and became the family choice horse for over twenty-years plus, leaving behind a legacy of many stories.

Dick had a mind of his own. When he was still young, Father took a horseback ride to his parents' home for the weekend. Only a few miles away from our homestead, Dick refused to go any further. Dick would only go one direction, the one toward his home. Father had to come back to our homestead with Dick.

Dick had bridge phobia, and I sometimes wondered if Father was somewhat to blame. Father harassed Dick at the Milk River bridge on Bagan Road by dangling an empty can off a fishing pole alongside the horse. Dick, thinking the bridge was breaking through, sprawled his feet widely.

A CHIMNEY FIRE WHEN ARTHUR WAS BORN

The year of 1915 had many new adjustments to the homestead operation, including the enlargement of the family. Brother Arthur was born on March 18 on an eventful day. In his excitement, Father rashly overheated the coal stove, resulting in a chimney roof fire. Thanks to the nearby water pond, and a ladder high enough to reach the roof, the fire was subdued with many pails of water, while Mother anguished giving birth to my younger brother. Thank God that Mrs. Wilhelm Schroeder was with us for the midwife ministry.

A PRICKLY "SIT"UATION

At a gathering of homesteaders, one of the fellows stepped on some wild cactus, which pushed through his shoe. He needed to sit down to remove the painful prick. While doing so, he sat down on some more cacti.

Getting up with a smile and half-muttering, he said to himself, "Never mind, before long I'll have all this cactus plowed out."

This was a stupendous statement, for there were thousands of Montana acres winking at his challenge.

"ABEKE"

My mother's name was Helen, but during her whole lifetime she went by "Lena." Mother called Father "Abram" or "Ubram" in Low German (*Plattdeutsch*). As I grew older, there arose a little difficulty between Sr. and Jr., and my name became "Abeke" on the farm to prevent confusion. Junior, when he did not want to come, could play ignorant. But when Senior was called, Junior's curiosity, as a naturally front-line watcher, would show up also.

Abeke might have thought: *It's what you learn after you know it all that counts.*

EARLY YEARS ON THE HOMESTEAD

Before there were enough fences, the livestock ran loose. Father enticed the tame horses with buckets of fresh ground feed, giving them samples. Over time, he was able to bring them further and further into the wild pastures. When he needed to round up the horses, Father would walk with a bucket of fresh ground feed so that the wind would carry the aroma to their nostrils. The horses would surround his bucket for samples as Father put on their halters.

FIRST TELEPHONE LINES

The community telephone finally made it close to our home when enough road fences were erected. At the twelve-mile corner (Bagan Road at Highway #2), there were about a dozen mostly homemade mailboxes. Father bought No 8, wire hanging it on low poles and stretched it to our home. For a short duration, Mother was asked to serve as telephone switch operator. It was a simple job, pulling some connecting switches to ring the party involved with some short and longer ringing.

FATHER'S EARLY BLACKSMITH SHOP

Father had built a beautiful blacksmith shop for himself. It was supplied with a crank-blower chimney forge, attached to a four-inch flue pipe. The building has a small chimney sticking out of the roof. The blower forge would turn blacksmith coal to white heat in a hurry. He supplied himself with a heavy anvil and a good supply of blacksmith hammers and a press drill set. He had long-handled tongs that I believe were homemade. He became skilled at manufacturing all the hardware for the wagon yokes that required hot-sand welding.

CHINOOK GROCERY STORES

Both general stores in Chinook, Canfield and O'Handling stores, knew about Father's big family, and they always sent a sack of candy for the family with him when he came to town for supplies. Father would often come home and share the happenings from the city.

Occasionally he had to stay overnight in Chinook, usually with other fellows who lodged in the delivery stables barn, and upon rare occasion at the Chinook Hotel. One night when he was staying in the delivery stables, he noticed a fellow entering the barn, sucking a big pipe. Father didn't trust his situation for fear the hay would be ablaze before long. Father returned home the next day exhausted with no sleep, although the horses had rested and been fed.

FATHER'S CURIOSITY

Another time, Father delayed himself from leaving Chinook . . . his curiosity overwhelmed him while cautiously watching a fellow hitching up two big wagons to three-team of horses (six horses). When he was ready to leave, the man lifted his long leatherette and gave a crack, but unfortunately the whip wrapped around his own neck. The lead horses became more and more confused and would not cooperate. To save the man from utter embarrassment or worse, Father helped him regain control of the situation. Father later wondered what the full outcome might have been had he not got involved.

Father did not need to relate such stories twice, while I ate candy from the grocery store. (I am now over seventy as I write this, and both the candy and story are still sweet.)

PANIC AT MILK RIVER BRIDGE COLLAPSE

Father got into a homesteader's life-and-death struggle, as did most homesteaders at one time or another. One cold February, a Chinook wind arrived, sending so much snow into streams that it raised many of the bridges. Father was returning from delivering two wagons of grain to the elevator in Chinook where he spent the night.

On his return trip, the deep-snow-thawed water had beat him to the bridge over Milk River. The bridge had collapsed. As father tried to make it across, one of the horses slipped on icy footing, and its harness became entangled, as it attempted to jump into the icy waters. Father went into the icy stream to loosen the harness of the fallen horse.

Many miles downstream, Father did salvage his horses and both wagons, but only one empty box. After much delay, he re-hitched the horses to the wagon and resumed his way home. Wet, cold, and exhausted, he found himself falling asleep while the horses were losing their way and wandering openly. Father awakened with a panic, unable to regain a sense of direction, with nothing familiar in sight. In his panic he stood up, driving at gallop speed, hollering cries: Lost! Help, Lost, Help!"

He nearly ran over a sod house; but at the last minute, seeing a faint light, he stopped. The owner of the home was kind enough to warm him up, loan him some dry long underwear, and corrected direction. He could hardly believe the man's direction but followed those orders and arrived back on the Bagan Road, regaining his equilibrium. Finally he got home, thanking God, that his life had been spared.

Man seated outside his humble soddy, early 1900s. Photo from the Fred Hultstrand and F.A. Pazandak collections

MODEL T FORD

One day Father came home with a 1916 Model T Ford. The fold top was up, and the plastic window lookouts had curtains that were fastened up. That was the first time in my life that I beheld something black so large. The whole thing was shining.

Father lost no time at his blacksmith shop to fix a heavy-duty hitch to the frame. Soon, with a two-wheel trailer loaded with three drums (55–66 gallons each) and other wares, he would go high speed downhill to compensate for the next upgrade or mud slopes. He had a breakdown with rear end gears, and had no choice but to take it all apart and install new parts.

In the process, he got confused as to which way the parts were to function, and he put it together wrong. When he started the motor, one wheel wanted to go forward, while the other wheel turned backward. He finally got it together correctly.

Father was an excellent blacksmith, but not outstanding as an automotive mechanic.

ELMER DRIVES AND FATHER MUST WALK

Elmer started to drive a Model T Ford at age eight. Father and Elmer drove to the Homestead for some sort of chores and, when they finished, Father asked Elmer to drive to the gate at the section line and wait for him. Elmer either did not understand or was simply overtaken with driving; because, after he got to the gate, he continued to drive all the way home to the Becker ranch and made Father walk four-plus miles home.

THE AVERY TRACTOR

Father's new Avery tractor was a health tonic and a source of pride and enjoyment the entire duration of his farming. It started good, winter and summer, and never broke down. In winter, the tractor stood at the north end of the two-story granary, facing the granary (southward) a short belt was on the big pulley, attached to a small feed grinder on the inside of the granary.

In winter we would run it with no water in the radiator, and keep it at idling speed, so it didn't heat up. When Father wasn't on the yard, my older brother Elmer, would squirt primer into the carburetor and grab that long straight-handle and give it a crank. Just one twist and *puff, puff.*

1918 photo of Abraham B Becker's 1911 Avery steam tractor.

I never heard what the World War One price tag was for the Avery but the 4-bottom plow cost $800. I remember Father sharpening those plow shares . . . showing off, demonstrating, and saying, "This big hammer makes big muscles."

$10,000. SCHMIDT CHECK

Mr. Jacob Schmidt, from Dolton, South Dakota, visited the Becker Montana Homestead. In his hand was a $10,000. check of earnest money. His visit was short, shrewd, and with skilled cleverness. Before he left, he had purchased the late Benjamin Buller Homestead, where both Lena (my mother) and Abeke were born. That "Good-bye" was a heartache and anguish of mind for dear Mother.

GRANDMOTHER BECKER

Another early visitor on the Homestead was Grandmother Susanna Becker. My father's parents: the Rev. (Heinrich) Benjamin and Susanna Becker were the pioneer pastors of the Evangelical Mennonite Brethren Church at Marion, South Dakota. Grandfather died early, but Grandmother lived until April 1, 1930. Years later, in 1984, I would identify over 1,200 decedents of my grandfather, Heinrich Benjamin Becker, and document them in a family tree.

BUILDING OF THE BIG CHURCH

The Evangelical Mennonite Brethren (Walla) Church was built in 1916. My father, Abraham Becker Sr., was young, robust, hale, and hearty at age thirty-two. He planked down $100. earnest money and volunteered to provide all transportation of the church constructional material to the jobsite.

He took his new Avery tractor and a train of five broad wagons to the Chinook, where he had these wagons loaded sky high with beams, planks, rafters, floor timber, two-by-fours, flooring nails, shingles, cement, and anything else needed for the church. When he got to the big hill with his train of fully loaded wagons, he played it safe, making two trips up the hill after unhooking three wagons for fear the loads would jackknife.

What a beautiful sanctuary the church had, especially for that time and location. It was forty feet wide by eighty feet long, with a large balcony, two front-door entries, one side entry, and a full basement. In the mid-1930s, this building was purchased by the Lutheran Congregation and moved to Chinook. It is still used as a testimony of Christian faith and labor of love.

Montana Evangelical Mennonite Brethren (Walla) Church

FATHER'S PLAYER PIANO AND THE PARTY LINE

Father was very musically inclined and, after the bumper wheat crop of 1914–15, he ordered a player piano for himself. It was still winter when it arrived at Chinook Depot, and he backed up his bobsled to the loading dock. When Father came into the Depot, one of the church fellows was pointing to a big upright phonograph, saying, "This in mine."

Father, standing by that enormous box, "his new piano," said, "And this is mine."

The fellows in the Depot, thinking him to be joking, were not about to cooperate with load lifting that heavy freight. Father had his big crowbar along and began to move that heavy freight to the door. Then they had a change of mind, where seeing is believing, and they helped him load it.

It was not long until father had a box of about sixty-five roller-records. How he enjoyed them! Usually he would accompany them with his violin and change off to his deep, pear-shaped, fretted-neck mandolin. He played both instruments well, either carrying the melody or cording music. He could also play his bugle with his mouth, and all three simultaneously. It was beautiful! In those days all the homesteaders were on the same phone line, commonly referred to as a "party line."

Father's church friends would ring the telephone line ten shorts, signaling announcement call that "Mr. Abraham Becker will serenade us with his music instruments." Those Montana snow-stormy nights made Father the first music broadcaster—before radio days.

Years later, his grandson, Tim Koehn, paid tribute to his ancestors by writing the song, "Party Line" about the music heard on Montana prairie during the homestead days.

Party Line
A long, long time ago on a farm in Montana
There lived a family I call my own
There was so much to do
So many chores they knew
but when evenin' came they played the party line

Choirs: Mama played the mandolin
Aunt Ida she would join right in
Playin' on that old tenner guitar
Uncle Abe he played the violin
Grandpa pumped his player piano
Playin' on the country party line

People called from miles around
Just to hear them play
Such a very happy sound in an old familiar way
They didn't call to put them down
They were the happiest folks around
Listening in on the country party line

And sometimes on a quiet night
I think of what a glorious sight
It must have been to see them playing there
A warm fire in the fireplace
I think I hear Amazing Grace
Playin' on the country party line

I hear my Moma playin' the mandolin
Aunt Ida she is joinin' in
Playin' on that old tenner guitar
Uncle Abe is playin' his violyn
Grandpa's pumpin' his player piano
Playin' on the country party line
I hear 'em playin' on the country party line
Oh they were playin' on the country party line

Music and lyrics by Tim Koehn

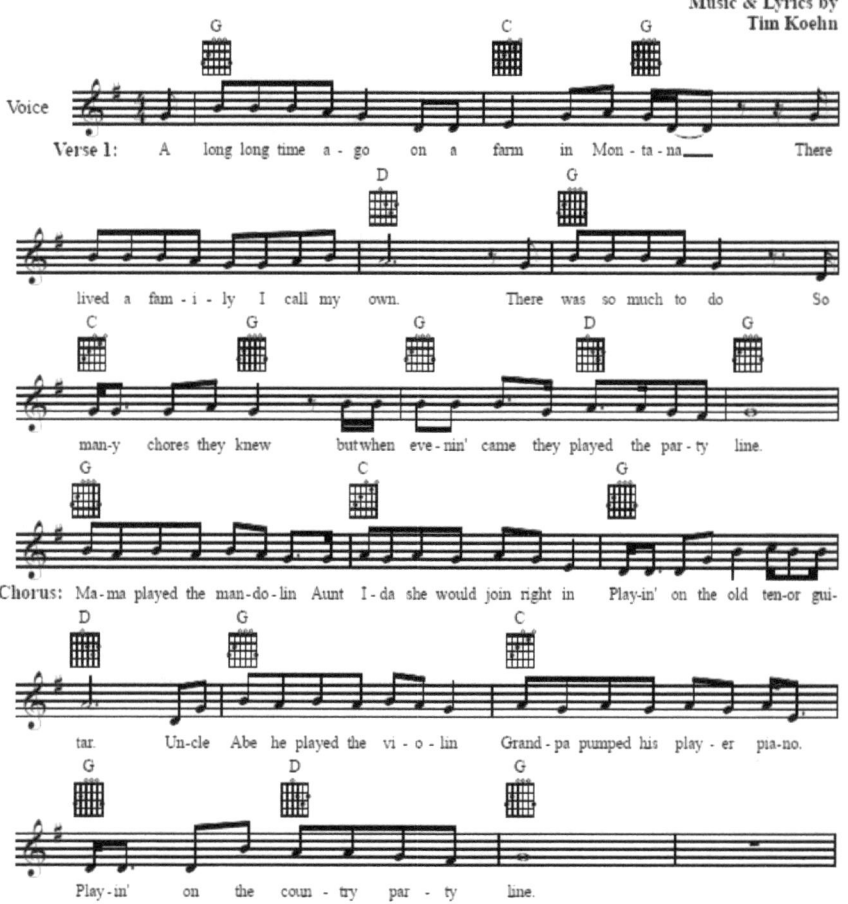

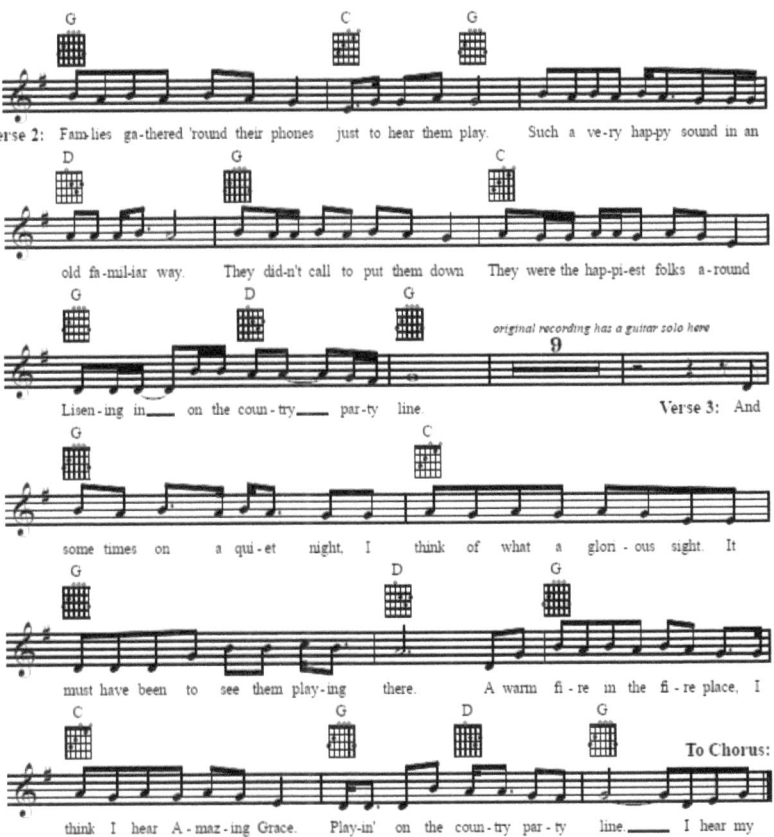

Final Chorus Lyrics :
Mama playing the mandolin, Aunt Ida she is joining in
Playin' on that old tenor guitar, Uncle Abe is playin' his violin
Grandpa's pumpin' his player piano, Playin' on the country party line
I hear 'em playin' on the country party line. Oh they were playin' on the country party line

SISTER IDA IS BORN

November 4, 1916, became a special day when Mother gave birth to sister Ida. Our large family was all born at home with the help of a midwife ministry, all that is except Ida, who was born at Zurich. Ida was born unexpectedly as Mother accompanied Father on a trip to Zurich, which is about ten miles east of Chinook.

Firstborn sister Bertha was only seven, and us being young, Father played mother cook and fried thick-sliced pork chops and eggs with much black pepper, which he happily served me. But one look at them—they were not like Mother had been preparing them for us youngsters. No doubt half emotionally upset . . . and Mother not at the table, I was in no mood nor able to swallow those black-peppered eggs. I sensed a disappointment in Father's voice, and he felt equally bad for me.

FIRST CHRISTMAS PROGRAM

First things in child's life are so precious. The first Christmas I remember on the homestead was the one where Father had been drilling me to memorize a Bible verse, and to recite it distinctly with a full voice. My recitation was Luke 2:14 in German, *"Ehre sei Gott in der Höhe, und Friede auf Erden, und den Menschen ein Wholgefallen"* (Glory to God in the highest, and on earth peace, good will toward men.)

When time came to go to the large church for the Christmas program, Father loaded us up in a bobsled full of hay, covered with a lovely horse-hair blanket. We children lay down flat and covered with another lovely blanket.

At the church, there were many rows of children and young people. The Christmas program was very long, during which time I believe I fell asleep on the front bench to the right. Then suddenly waking up with a panic, thinking I had been called on to recite my verse, I jumped to my feet, ran to the platform, threw my head back, I believe my eyes closed, hollering off my recitation.

Now the German Mennonites are not much given to express themselves in public audibly; however, I do remember the superintendent-chairman speaking with emotion to my mother. I remember asking her what the man said.

Mother answered me, saying: "The man said, 'there is a preacher in the making,'" which became a true prophecy.

MY FIRST CHRISTMAS GIFT

The same Christmas season, my older brother, Elmer, received a tricycle, and I received a four-piece trainset. That beautiful little train would intrigue any child, and my little brother Arthur was not to be blamed for having his eyes fixed on it. A rumpus broke out between me and my little brother every time I put my hand on my Christmas gift. Father tried to negotiate the friction by dividing two-pieces for each of us. But that was not a train to me . . . so I just sat there and looked. I sorta remember later that Father tried to have me enjoy the train, but I only remember it as a "hands-off" train.

HOMESTEAD HUMOR

The homestead had a closet chemical tank toilet (big bucket) with a seat cover, and ventilated with a four-inch pipe. For some reason or another, it was not moved to the Becker homestead; but I remember that it resurfaced for the 1942 auction sale. Father felt forlorn and wretched with the farm sale prices at the sale; however, he came home from the sale full of laughable incidents.

The auctioneer started that 3-Farm Sale with that home-chamber-toilet, and some very laughable remarks. When he had everyone laughing then he proceeded with the sale. (More about the sale later).

Sister Ida learned to talk at age two. Sitting at the evening table on Father's lap, he coaxed little Ida to speak English. He imposed on her . . . "open your mouth any old way, and speak English." So she opened and twisted her mouth to utter anything that she could frame. So she says: "Wire, prince."

That's all the words I remember these many years hence. But I remember how Father and Mother had a great laugh, because "wire," in German is *draht* and prince "ruler."

LEARNING TO COUNT TO FIVE

Father was fond of homemade ice cream. One day on the homestead, while Father was cranking the ice cream freezer in the basement, he taught the children to count with him while he made the cranks. So I learned to count to five in German, so he says: "Abeke, you run upstairs and count on your fingers to five for Mother."

I continued to count all the way up the stairway . . . mixing up my numbers as I went. When I counted for Mother, my numbers were out of consecutive order. She laughed but did not correct me, and I also was aware that I was mixed up.

Then Mother says: "Abeke, you go back downstairs, and learn your lesson over again with Father."

The second training was not as joyous, but I learned. Soon I was using my new skill to count cows, heifers, steer, and calves. I knew exactly if any were missing.

HORSE PRIDE TRADED FOR MULE PRIDE

With the Avery tractor coming to the Becker farm, something brought another radical change. Maybe it was a hidden display of pride but, at any rate, Father sold and traded his horses and bought four mules. The gray one of them was quite young, and it was as tall as it was long. One day it wandered away eastward four or five miles.

Cousin Sam was in their field, harrowing with a multiple team, standing on the evener, to which the single-trees harness tugs were fastened. Watching his operation cautiously, he did not behold the Becker long-eared gray beast coming across the field toward him. No doubt Uncle Jakes had not been near long-eared mules, and thus took it for a wild beast phobia. Sam, losing his standing balance, fell off in front of the harrows and got a good rolling-dragging, mars and scratching.

Father often hitched up a team of those mules and proceeded to the city of Chinook. But he was not able to complete his journey because of the stubborn mules. He made it to Bagan Road and Highway 2, where gateway poles stood on either side. Here close to the road, was a new open animal hole (sizable) . . . and the mules, being very suspicious, were instantly framed up with illusion, although unreal. Their minds were riveted not to cross that gateway passage.

Father tried to back them through and tried putting gunny sacks over their heads—even his own overcoat . . . no way, nothing doing. Finally, Father had to tie those mules to the wagon, walk the three miles west to Chinook and back again, carrying a few groceries. On his return trip to his home, Father's mind was somersaulting with agitation, and he determined to buy back his previous heavy horses. Father found that homesteading horses were in demand, and his old horses were not for sale. The only things Father could find to replace those stubborn mules were partial bronco horses.

Of course Father still had Nellie, Frannie, and young Dick. Dick was never for sale . . . he died of old age (1935–36) in South Dakota.

Before we left Montana, Father had bought a teammate for Dick. His name was "Jim" from the same studhorse, thus the same color (Indian Trotter). Unfortunately, Jim had been improperly halter-broken and never accepted a correction. When it was necessary to lead him, you had to almost drag him. The faster you needed to travel, the more Jim slagged back. If it could be calculated, Jim's frictional resistance cost the Becker family barrels of gasoline in wasted energy.

A NIGHT AUTOMOBILE ACCIDENT AND SUICIDE

Bagan Road Junction at Highway 2 (three miles East of Chinook) has a gruesome history. This location was the same location where Father's mules panicked several years before.

On a snowstorm scary night, a man driving his auto too fast to negotiate the turn of the corner of Bagan road unto Highway 2 upset his vehicle and severely broke the bones in one of his legs. This road was seldom used and there were no other travelers that snowy evening. The man was able to crawl a full mile toward Chinook, dragging his broken leg before wearing out. Overcome with confusion, he reached for his pocketknife and cut his throat, bleeding to death.

Upon hearing the sad story, Father was deeply moved with grief and pity, having gone through fearful woes himself in the same location. He also had a deep burden and concern for the man's family.

THE TINIEST PERMANENT VISITOR

June 13, 1918, brought excitement to the Homesteader Becker Family. The tiniest baby, weighing in between two-and-a-half and three pounds, a new baby sister Olga arrived. Mrs. Schroeder was there again for midwife duties, and she came to me later in the day, saying "Abeke, you have a *kleina* baby *Schwester* (sister) Come, you want to see it?"

Madam Schroeder led me to the side of the bed of Mother. Maybe they were not able to lift the frail little tot for my inspection, but I was young and small standing there and saw nothing. Yes, I saw Mother's arm, and maybe the tiny tot in between. But neither Mother nor nurse Schroeder discerned that I really had not observed the newcomer.

Deeply bewildered/embarrassed, I very slowly backed away from Mother's bed, saying nothing, nor answering questions they asked me. Not many days later, when I had to rock the cradle, it finally convinced me, that there was "somebody new in the family."

Sister Ida grew up very strong in body and beautiful stature; but in her infancy, she was double-jointed, feet sorta sprawled out to stand. So really, we had two babies and two baby cribs at the same time.

There was a crank-spring, self-rocker crib and a round-oval hand-push crib rocker. Elmer and I were trained early to give Mother a hand with these two cribs. Elmer remembers laying on his back while kicking the crib with his feet, instead of standing and using his hands gently. I rocked that crib endlessly to Mother's smile of satisfaction.

A NEW WASH MACHINE

One day I observed a new wash machine. It had a handle for the hand, plus a foot crank to use simultaneously for easier operation. With so many children, Mother learned to do many chores quickly. To use the new wash machine, she carried steaming water in a big copper boiler heated on the cook stove to fill this new machine. While she was away, I was closely inspecting it and found the big-round wooden drain-plug. I assumed that stopper had a purpose, so I gave it a yank and sure enough it came right out. Low and behold so did the steaming hot water.

Realizing my mistake, I instantly pushed that stopper back in place, but the boiling hot water took the skin right off my tender hand and pealed it like a scalded chicken. Mother was gifted with a nurse instinct and quickly saved me from the painful situation.

STICKY FLY RIBBON AND FLY POISON

During these early homesteading days, an all-around new product appeared, icky fly ribbon and fly poison in beautiful green containers. My older brother Elmer got into the new containers and drank some of the poison. Soon he became violently sick. Mother soon observed that some of the new fly poison had been robbed of its contents. She lost no time and quickly poured milk down Elmer's throat. He heaved up a mess of green contents. Dr. Mother's fees were always free . . . more later.

SIGNING OF THE ARMISTICE

Our father, Mr. Abraham B. Becker, was in alignment for the draft in the World War I Army. He was age thirty-four, and the father of six children. The circle of his operation was sprawling out in family circle, church life, and farm activity—hard to eclipse. He was conscientious about right and wrong. Winter was ready to step in with the approach of November.

Father had day and night anxiety, and was no doubt eating and sleeping poorly. I remember Father and Mother whispering together. He was given to showing distress in his face. I knew something was wrong. Then out of the blue sky rang the news of the signing of the Armistice on November 11, 1918.

I do not exactly remember whether the draft fellows threw their hats into the air. But I wish there was a tape recording to share with us the verbalization of Father's comrades: "The Great War is over." With the Armistice behind him, also came the hope of a new tomorrow. Father's dream was to make it rich.

THE LORD'S PROTECTION

As I write this manuscript, my mind is afloat with the many times that I could have been snatched out of existence. While very young, we had a horse dying with cramps, lying on its side. No one around and my curiosity running wild, I stepped up close to take a good look when suddenly the sick horse gave a long-swing kick, hitting me in the head . . . I still have the scar.

On another day, some men were gathering stones into a wagon box when my curiosity pushed me to see how the pile looked from inside the wagon box. I was climbing the tall wagon wheel spokes when suddenly the horses were signaled to move forward. I grabbed the box wall with both hands, holding on for dear life as I was drug for a good distance right in front of that rolling wagon wheel. My "curiosity" caused my parents a lot of grief . . . but I am still glad I was born with it.

A HALF SECTION AND A WHOLE SECTION MORE LAND

Our parents were friends with the Dick Schultz, who had homesteaded the half-section west of the Rev. Henry C. Unruh. Dick Schultz was dying on his couch with stomach cancer, so Father and Mother did all they could for this dear couple. I remember joining my parents and the loathsome-odious smell of the gallon spittle canteen Dick used. This was very disturbing to me as a child and I remember thinking my father and mother must really love this man to help minister in his time of affliction. Having now been a pastor and evangelist for many years, I have since been to many a bedside of various afflictions, and I am thankful for this first observation of love.

Through Father's kindness, he took over the responsibility for the Schultzs' two quarters of land. We plowed one quarter and pastured the south quarter. These two quarters lay parallel (one mile) eastside Bagan Road. The Becker Reservoir ranch lay a mile further north, parallel (one mile) on the west side of Bagan Road.

1918 WAS A BUSY YEAR

1918 must have been a very busy year for Father. His vision to build a water dam alongside a big hill that ended with a butte-cut bank at the north end was brilliant. A sizable valley from the south with water flowing northward was filling the barricade with water before it fell into the Coulee, which ran from the east to west. The reservoir should be considered an engineering success for its day.

He laid out the farm design and dug a cellar basement for a two-story granary and another one for a bungalow house. He also dug a large cistern below our porch, plastered it, and made a proper lid to cover it.

Father fell from a barn during young manhood, and he feared climbing after that. He hired help to build his high granary and worked alongside as sawman.

During all this time, little coffee-can-sized sister, Olga, was putting on the pounds. She had good sleeping hours, and Elmer and I were kept busy rocking her cradle. Family and friends marveled how Mother could preserve the life of such a small baby. She was indeed a doctor-nurse-mother.

When the granary building was finished, we painted it gray and used it for a house dwelling while the bungalow was being completed.

MOVING TO THE NEW RANCH, 1919

Excitement was at a boiling stage prior to moving day to the new ranch in the winter of 1919. Father had been talking to us youngsters as though we were young men. He made statements like, "Abeke, when we move, you can drive the cows."

I was only five, and the move was four miles.

The moving train arrived at the new farm sight and so had the curiosity of Abeke. I immediately began to inspect the new house and granary basement/cellar. I then climbed the wall that had two-by-four steps up into a dormer in the barn. Having never fallen before, I had no fear. When I got ready for the down climb, I lost my balance and fell nine feet to the hard floor below, completely knocking the wind out. Unable to breathe, I stumbled toward the house, finally catching my breath. I now respected heights differently.

PORCUPINE EXCITEMENT

After church dismissed one day, several men were lingering and talking together when an unusual animal crawled into the motor department of one of their vehicles. Willie Schroeder took a thin fencepost to shove the animal out of the engine area.

As soon as the animal hit the ground, the men started shouting, "A porcupine," and immediately I was a front-line watcher. Soon I was shoved away from the shooting needles as the ground turned gray and white with countless needles. It was another one of those unforgettable memories.

WORSHIP, FELLOWSHIP, ENCOURAGEMENT, AND A GOOD LAUGH

In addition to the blessings we received from worshipping together, the fellowship in the big Mennonite church provided homesteaders some much-needed emotional support and encouragement, and often a good laugh. So it was one Sunday following the service when an unusually high wind ripped the hats off the men who stood outside. Those hats blew in overdrive fashion, rolling on the prairies, and soon were out of reach of even the fastest runner.

One of the homesteaders said, "Here in Montana, we never run after our own hats, we just turn about and catch the hat that is rolling to meet us."

"A merry heart doeth good like a medicine." —Proverbs 17:22.

WHERE'S THE WATER?

One hot summer day Father was plowing, and Mother felt impressed that poor Pa was probably getting thirsty. She filled a shiny half-gallon syrup pail with drinking water and sent me to take it to Father working in the field. There were a lot of thistle pricks and thorns, and I was bare foot, so travel was slow and cautious.

When I finally made it to Father, he smiled at me, appreciating Mother's thoughtfulness and kindness, but his countenance changed when I had handed him the syrup pail. "Where's the water?" he asked. I had no answer.

"Did you fall?"

"No!"

Not doubting my sincerity any longer, he lifted the small pail again, and facing the sun, he beheld a tiny rusty hole. The water had dripped out drop-by-drop without me realizing it.

I have used this experience as an illustration, explaining how some people lose their close walk with the Lord through what I call "the peril of the gradual."

BUTTER CHURN CURIOSITY

Mother purchased a new barrel-type, butter churn that had a beautiful lid with a glass peephole, so it was possible to see when buttermilk would wash the glass dark, indicating it was done. We were able to make more butter than we needed and sold some to neighbors.

One day as I cranked the churn, it did not take long, and the buttermilk separated, and the peephole indicated finished! I was amazed at how soon it was finished and was curious to see if the butter rolled up into little balls or possibly one big lump. My inspection was brief, thinking I heard footsteps.

In my hurry to cover my tracks, I had forgotten to pull the lid tight, and I overturned the barrel, dumping the whole contents on that new floor. There was no way for me to salvage the situation, so out of the door I went, sneaking away down a pathway to a nearby ravine.

Father had seen me, but he was unaware of the mess I had made, and he was only amazed at my peculiar departure. I was peeping over the edge of the hill, awaiting the discovery of my disastrous casualty when, sure enough, Mother found it. Mother called Father, and he knew exactly where I was hibernating.

He did not call for me but simply walked all the way to where I was hiding. He took a hold of my upper arm below my shoulder, and we walked together silently. When we got to the mess I had made, Father asked me, "Is this your mess?"

I answered, "Yes."

"Did Mother give you permission to open the churn?" he asked.

"No." I had earned a double punishment; I got a stinging whipping and was put into the cellar-jail, to think it over.

The new cellar had a ground shelf, shoulder-high for fruit jars, and a lower place for miscellaneous items that had dried fruits stored on it. I don't know what possessed me; but I started helping myself to a picnic of dried prunes. I did not want to spit out the prune pits as it would tattle tale on me, so I kept them in my mouth and kept feeding myself more.

There was an open basement window and, when I turned to look out it, I observed two piercing eyes, as though they were lit up with bright fire. Instantly screaming with all my might, I ran up the stairs. Finding the door locked, I pushed with all my strength, and I cracked that double door. Father and Mother rushed to the cellar door, where I was roaring calamitously, but they could not unfasten the lock, because of the intense pressure I was giving the door.

Finally they succeeded in opening it. "What happened?" they asked me.

I could not answer because my mouth was overloaded with fruit pits. Wise Mother observing something, stuck her finger into my mouth and with one swipe over my tongue, pulled out a handful of the mess. Father then, shaking me, asked in German, "Child, what is the matter?" (*Kind, was ist los?*)

Trembling, I muttered, "There is a man downstairs—in the corner."

Father and Mother cautiously walked downstairs for an inspection. They found a big cat sitting there on the shelf, back of the fruit jars, no doubt amazed at the peculiar circus it had just witnessed. They returned to persuade me: "That there is no burglar-tramp downstairs . . . that it was only a big old tom cat, with shining eyes, looking at me."

This episode is now seventy years old, but if it was to live to reach the age of Methuselah, it will linger and tarry with me.

LIGHTNING STRIKES THE GRANARY CHIMNEY

In the summer of 1920, heavy storm clouds were moving in as I carried two heavy plowshares for Father. Mother was in the granary, filling a big bottle tank with kerosene for her oil cooker when suddenly a severe lightning bolt struck the granary. The electric shock threw Mother backward, flat on her back.

Our big dog Prince must have sensed weather danger, as he had entered the house and crawled under the big cook stove. Prince may have felt sparks of electricity when the thunderbolt struck the granary and he came out yipping-barking and bit a rubber ball of mine and punctured it. What a narrow escape it was for all of us. Thank God for sparing us.

MONTANA JUNE BERRIES

One beautiful summer day in the dry year of 1920, two women, Mrs. Acres and Mrs. Johnson, arrived at our home. Mother and I hurriedly hitched up Dick to the single-shaft top buggy, and the four of us went berry-picking together. Mother and I filled a five-gallon cream can and several other containers.

Mother had packed a picnic lunch for us, at which time one of the women joked, saying, "What a great time we three cows and one bull are having here in these wilds."

WHOOPING COUGH

It was harvesting and thrashing time, and I was coming down with a bad case of whooping cough. I could see Abe Peter's big steam engine slowly moving south at about two miles per hour on Bagan Road. It seemed like a very long time for the outfit to arrive at our home. Mother was furiously working, preparing a "thrashers-gang" dinner, something she was good at.

That night I coughed until my stomach felt like it would come out my throat. I vomited on a nice blanket, and Mother came in and cleaned it up, saying nothing. Soon I soiled the second and third beds also. Now these three beds were originally set up for the thrasher fellows, who had to wait. This was a hard day for Mother!

MENNONITE CONFERENCE GUEST CHURCH

1920 was a year of overload and crises. The General Conference of the Evangelical Mennonite Brethren was scheduled at our Church that year. One Sunday morning on our way to church, Mother noticed that many of the church families had painted their cars in preparation for the conference. A few days later, Father came home from Chinook with a supply of paint and brushes. How he did work to clean the soiled Model T that he had used for a truck the last five years! Father scrubbed that old Ford by a little dam and then painted it. He did a great job in restoring that weathered Ford. Beautiful!

When the conference started, poor Mother was unable to attend a single day, not even that special Sunday. The family was made ready to go to church, and Father says, "Abeke, you will have to stay with Mother, she needs you."

He then handed me his box of harmonicas and told me to play them to offset my disappointment, as he knew I dearly loved Sunday school. Poor Mother had stayed home from the conference for safety's sake, and for respectability's sake. She was to deliver a twelve-pound Walter in a few days. Mother sat there and said in German, *"Ich bin ein angebundener hund."* (I am a tied-up dog).

Chinook, Montana, was so far from the other states attending the conference. So many had come, including friends and uncles and aunts from Washington and Canada who Mother would not see again. A few friends stopped by our home and among them was Mother's favorite aunt, Lidtke, from Canada.

Heavy rain caused the Choteau Coulee to be muddy everywhere. I remember how impressed Mother's aunt was with her niece Lena. Mother had taken a butcher knife to the edge of the garden field and cut a big green Russian thistle for a door mat. It was moist enough to do the trick and worked wonderfully. This same cloud burst filled the reservoir for the first time.

THE BIG RESERVOIR FILLS AND OVERFLOWS

The rain not only filled the empty new dam, it overflowed it. Father had improvised a wooden board spillway however it was inadequate. The rain overflow washed those boards out and tore away much dam ground. Father went to work with a sand shovel at the top of the dam, maybe using some the boards for a wall and was able to salvage the dam. The dam has now withstood seventy years of weather.

The reservoir brought many joys to a prairie land that suffered for water. The water it contained was even used by some of the community who hauled it to their farms.

Father loved to hunt ducks, and Mother would fry them for dinner. Our dog, Shep, would swim the deep river and fetch the killed ducks.

CHINOOK LADY HURTS MOTHER'S FEELINGS

We sometimes would receive visitors from Chinook to the Becker ranch. One such lady visitor sat looking at Mother and said something like, "Huh? Another Baby?"

At that point, Mother had three boys and three girls, and the lady must have thought *What's the matter with you, isn't that enough?*

Mother, just grinned and silently took it all in.

Mother was overloaded with many responsibilities. She had just recently clipped the long black hair from sisters, Ida and Olga. They were cut straight fashion, and I didn't like the looks of them. I wonder if the lady in that "self-starter" car was thinking about those queer haircuts of my sisters when she made her condescending comments to Mother.

WALTER IS BORN

August 15, 1920, came, and we children were taken to Henry Coolie Unrauh. Sometime later when we were to be brought back to our home and Mr. Unrauh looked right at me and told us that we had a twelve-pound brother waiting for me at home. Baby pounds did not have much meaning to me, but I remember it. There was evidence of Mother's bleeding, and an environment that spoke for itself, that Mother had been through a very difficult time with the birth.

THOSE FOUR MULES: LAST GOODBYE

Father hired himself out to header the wheat for John F. Tieszen. Instead of taking the mile section roads, probably five, six miles, he cut across country, which was much hillier than Father had expected. Tugging the machinery up those sandy hills became nearly impossible had it not been for those mules. The mules practically got on their knees, pulling so hard, and succeeded. If they could be motivated, they could really pull hard.

Years before, they would not cross that animal hole, three miles east of Chinook; but they must have repented and tugged these sandy hills. They seemingly now liked their boss, Mr. Becker, but it was too late, they soon were gone for good.

MOVING HOMESTEAD BARN TO BECKER RANCH

The moving of the Beckers from the original homestead site to the Becker ranch was both an event and a process. It was a little over four miles. After the family, household goods, cattle, blacksmith shop tools and machinery were moved, Father proceeded to move the cattle and horse barn. It was during these days that several horses were pastured at the homestead. Father got up on horseback and drove the other horses into a corral.

A studhorse became upset and severely kicked Father's ankle. This was a serious accident for Father because this very foot had once before been broken badly. I do not remember the doctor's care, except that it did not slow Father down with the moving process.

The foot, of course, was heavily bandaged. It was wrapped in gunny sacks for extra warmth and protection; but he kept right on working and moving that barn. He crawled on his knees and mounted his Avery tractor. He raised the barn, using heavy Avery jacks and placed it on long moving beams. He then successfully drug the barn to his second farm.

PLUMP FRANA TURNED SKINNY

The homestead continued to be used to pasture range horses during winter months. There was a small water dam there that froze over in winter. The horses would use their front feet to peel back the snow off the buffalo grass and graze the grass below the snow. The horses became husky and plump, and their fur became long with flush hair for the winter.

In late winter, Father brought home a black horse called Frana. The open prairie had spoiled this Frana, and she didn't like to be cooped up in the barn, and she refused to drink for days upon days. But the day came when she became so thirsty, that she drank and drank, and some more and some more. This radical change upset her whole digestive system, and she developed a severe case of loose bowels. To make matters worse, she developed a cough. You didn't dare hitch her up to the haywrack wagon or buggy.

She had lived under the cold sky, eating grass with snow, and was a beauty to behold in her black plump fur coat. Now she was sick, thin as a rail, and as pitiful of a piece of frame paneling. You could have called her "Framee instead of Frana."

HORSES OUTWIT FATHER

The demand for horses was great, and large work horses were especially hard to find. Father bought and traded horses as another source of income. On the homestead, Father had been able to allure his gentle horses with ground feed aroma... but this was not possible on the ranch, so Father thought up new approach. His big reservoir had a fence going right into the water, creating a wonderful place to corner those horses.

Much to his surprise, those horses plunged into that twenty-foot-deep water and swam across. There were infant colts with the herd, and they likewise swam across with just their heads sticking out, and their tail floating behind them. (When did they learn to swim?)

BOYS RODEO SPECTACLE

Two young mares were permitted to roam free in the yard. It was getting cold, and they would feed by haystacks. It was fun to smash your face in their warm fur-long hairs.

Older brother Elmer and I were young, naïve, and unafraid cowboys in the making. These young horses acted so gentle and tame to us, so we had the idea, "Let's ride these ponies." I put a halter on one of them and persuaded it to walk. And sure enough it walked around a little and stopped nearly where I got on. Elmer did the same with the other one; however she took a short turn and started bucking. Elmer landed safely on the ground with only his pride hurt.

My curiosity unsatisfied. More Fun! Second Round. So again I led mine to my favorite launching stage and jumped back on the horse. This time the mare was immediately frightened and took off with a panic at high speed, making a big circle on the yard, heading back for a passage between that stack and blacksmith shop where there was new ice on the ground.

At high speed, the mare could not negotiate the sharp corner turn and smacked into that building sideways. The crash of the horse into the building knocked me off with a bang resembling a shot rabbit. My groin was stretched severely, and I was sore for supper time.

After supper, I was asked to carry the oil lantern for the barn chores. Elmer and said nothing about the strange/dangerous young horse ride. But by now I could not walk normal, so I compensated, shifting my whole body to make steps.

Father was still not aware of the whole affair and thought that I was acting up. He demanded that I walk uprightly, and I answered, "I can't."

I then had to share the unbelievable story of how I was injured.

PURDY DESTROYS OUR BUGGY

One day Father came riding up on his Avery tractor while Purdy stood by hitched to the single shaft buggy. When he left on the tractor, he pulled the throttle open, and a big puff of smoke came out the chimney. Purdy was peeping around the house corner and saw the smoke cloud and the Avery tractor coming toward the house. She took off like a scared rabbit, pulling the buggy at high speed, shattering one of the buggy wheels completely off, and leaving the buggy irreparable. The loss of that buggy was often felt.

PRINCE THE AIREDALE

The family dog was an Airedale, and his name was Prince. He was a large terrier with a hard and wiry coat. His face, chest, and feet were brown, and his body black with a short stubby tail. He was friendly and would not think of biting an animal on the farm.

One day Prince went through the open back door into the basement of the two-story granary. I found him asleep on the cool dirt floor. Beside the granary was a long fishing pole, and I don't know what possessed me; but I quietly picked up that long fishing pole, stuck it through one of the side windows, and poked old Prince.

He woke up and grabbed that fishing pole chewing a good length of it to pieces in a hurry.

SHEP AND THIRTY DEAD CHICKENS

One fall day, Father came home with a beautiful collie, and his name was "Shep" There was a long low house at the Becker ranch, and we used half of it for a sizable blacksmith shop; and the other half was used for a chicken barn. It was cold the first night, and Father put Shep in the warm chicken barn for his first night. The next morning when Father walked into the chicken barn to greet his new collie; what did he find, but thirty of his big Plymouth Rock, four and five-pounder chicken hens dead.

This was a great loss to us, and Father was overtaken with a deep disappointment and flooding anger. He abruptly picked up a heavy two-foot-long club and grabbed Shep by the neck with the other hand. Father put a heavy Plymouth Rock dead chicken over Shep's nose, and he clubbed away. Father grabbed as many dead hens as he could reach. That was the worst nose-pounding a dog ever got, and Shep very well understood what it was all about. Immediately following this, he was as friendly as he could be, and we all felt sorry for him with his puffed-up face. He learned his lesson; never again did he chase a chicken.

Shep became good at handling ranch horses and cattle. He knew how to avoid kicks while herding the most-stubborn farm animals.

DOG BECOMES A LION

Shep had long hair and being such a hardworking dog, Father decided to cool him, so he sheared his back, belly, and thinned his tail, but left a bush at the end of it, making him look very much like a lion. Neighbors and friends laughed at the lion the Beckers had at their place. He nearly passed for real.

Late February in 1924, while two railroad freight cars were loaded with cattle and horses and farm households, Shep traveled 1,000 miles by rail to Dolton, South Dakota. Father and Shep remained warm-hearted friends. The sad parting day came in December 1924. The Becker family enjoyed a chicken dinner, and the chicken bones were shoved together with the other kitchen leftovers. And Shep being hungry, ate too fast, chewing on those chicken bones when a sliver lodged deep in his throat. Father observing the difficulty, loaded the dog in his Model T Ford and made a trip to Bridgewater to the dentist. He carried Shep up a long stairway. The dentist examined the dog's throat, saying it was beyond him to help the dog.

"SPUNKY BILL" ZOOMS HOME WITHOUT ME

Mr. George Class was a bachelor who lost one arm. He raised potatoes, and I believe that he made whisky from them. George asked my father for a low-wheeled wagon with an ankle-box; and he asked if I could pull the wagon with our horse team. I had been driving Nelly and Frana during harvest the last two summers so Dad gave permission. Mr. Class lived several miles away. When we arrived, we dug and gathered potatoes for two days, and he promised me two silver dollars for each day, not bad for a youngster. He promised he would pay me after I hauled some wheat to Chinook for him.

Several days passed. One evening I had gathered the cattle from fields. I was riding "Bill," a high-spirited horse with beautiful long neck hair that would wave at you as you rode in the wind. I never could ride Bill bareback; for he was too tall for me to get on, and Bill was always saddled with an Army saddle, which appeared small on Bill. This Army saddle of course was equipped with foot stirrups, but they fit a long man's foot, not the young boy I was at that time. To accommodate my short legs, there were additional leather rings for the proper length for my short feet.

I possessed telescopic vision in those days and could see, several miles up the Bagon Road, that two wagons were tied together with a double team of horses pulling the rig. Without a doubt, I knew at once it to be Mr. George Class coming back from the Chinook Elevators and that he had four silver dollars in his pocket for me.

I was very excited, and I threw my hands up into the sky above me and shouted, "Whoopee" there come my long-awaited four silvers. Much to my surprise, spunky Bill leaped forward so furiously that it threw me backward on the horse; however, my feet were still in the upper leather stirrups. It was amazing how long I kept my equilibrium bouncing on the rear end of spunky Bill.

Finally my feet were free from the upper leather stirrups, and I rolled like a basketball over Bill's tail into those flying rear hind legs, rolling as I hit the hard ground amidst some rocks. I never did discern whether my skull above my left eye was kicked by a hoof or it hit one of those rocks on the ground; but I knew it hit something very hard.

I quickly got myself together and back on my feet; with my first thought being, *where is spunky Bill?* I spotted him galloping in overdrive, with his head straight up, and his long mane waving in the air from side to side. My father and mother had just spied spunky Bill speeding faster every gallop, but without a rider.

Father gave the Model T a crank, jumped in, and drove it in high gear up the cattle trail to where he saw me in the distance walking toward home. "What happened, Abeke? What happened Abeke?"

Seeing the Model T driving so furiously, I instantly knew there would be questions, *what do I say* . . . embarrassed to tell the truth about excitement . . . whoopee over those silver dollars, that I was anticipating from George Class.

Having just enough time to envision my predicament, Satan by now had perverted my mind, and blinded me, filling me with lies, so I told Father that as I was closing that long wire gate, spunky Bill turned about and the wire touched his hind legs, whereupon spunky Bill kicked at a distance, knocking my skull open above my left eye. (I still have the scar)

Mother dressed the wound beautifully.

Years later, 1933, when I thoroughly got "saved," and dug up every confession that bothered me, I confessed this dark ugly lie to my father.

BOBSLED ENVY

Father built a canopy for the bobsled that provided great protection when he took his family to church in bad weather. It had a slide door on the right side, a glass window in front, and a three-inch hole for the lines and a fishing pole whip.

After church one Sunday, Father lost no time to raddle that fishing pole through the bunghole, while Bill and Daog were trotting stately in overdrive speed. It was a sight to see with Daog's long white neck straight forward, and Bill's dark-gray neck nearly straight up, with his mane waving in the wind, and the family all protected inside the canopy Father had built. It didn't take long to drive the half-mile northward and mile westward, while the church people still stood outside church all watching us enviously.

FRANK THE BUCKSKIN (A TRAINED ROPER)

I often feared that Father thought Abeke was too young to handle spunky Bill at nine years of age. After a farm sale, Father came home with a beautiful buckskin, three-quarter-size horse. "Frank" was gentle and highly trained. I took a liking to Frank, and so did the mosquitoes, by the million. His buckskin neck was so loaded that they were pushing each other out of the way, so they could get to him.

I rode Frank bareback on my maiden trip several miles along the Choteau Coulee to round up the ranch cattle. To me, it was like driving a new race car. I was riding at gallop speed, approaching the cattle, when I shouted something while swinging my hand. Frank suddenly put on the brakes on and stopped short with a turnabout while I floated over his head, landing hard on the ground. I hurt all over and it was hard to remount and finish my maiden excursion.

Arriving safely home, Father met me, smiling, and asks, "Well how was the ride, Abeke?"

"O, Father, a woeful experience," and I related the whole weary ordeal. I could tell that Father was still skeptic to believe my fairy tale.

The next evening arrived. I wanted to test Frank out again, but this time twisted my left hand tight into Frank's mane and shouted more softly, yet raising my hand; and sure enough, Frank stopped dead in his tracks again. Arriving home, I related this ordeal also. Father knew that I was not daydreaming, so the next evening he snuck away himself to find out for himself.

Returning home he approached me humbly and confirmed that indeed Frank has a funny habit. Father went back to complain to the original owner of Frank and let him know what had happened.

The previous owner said, "Mr. Becker, you should have listened closer to the auctioneer because he plainly announced that Frank was gentle, but a trained roper."

Well that explained it.

Frank loved farm life best when he was by himself, but when you put a heavy harness on him and hitched him to any machinery, he would panic with some type of phobia. He would get bucky, and sometimes he even laid down flat and played dead. One time when he did this, Father tied wire around his upper lip, and Mother poured water into his ears, all to none avail.

I think Frank was ready to speak Balaam's Dunky language, "Don't torture me any further, I was born and trained as a roper, and I give my best . . . but this grain header is not for me."

Frank, the roper knew me as barefoot lad at age nine and ten. "Now sixty-five years later, I still have sweet memories of him and miss him!

BOUNTIFUL HARVEST

Father had bought a new binder for his first bountiful thirty-seven-bushel-per-acre harvest we experienced the first years on the homestead;

but I do not remember it being used at all during the next five years on the Becker ranch. Then good crops came again in 1922 and 1923.

The binder header would cut a twelve-foot-wide strip of grain. When it was cutting, it had no mercy on you. Grain kept falling from that eight or ten-foot elevator into the barge where brother Elmer and I would trade off driving the barge wagon while the other one would shove and stack the heavy grain. Father was very aware of the hard task, and he would alternate the speed, gearing the cut grain to fall from the front of the barge onward to the back, which was a great help.

One time when I was driving the barge wagon, I dropped one of the team's lines out of my hand. Being embarrassed and frightened, I waited a short time doing nothing, but soon raised one hand with the line, and the other hand high-empty. Father instantly knew my predicament and said: "WHOA!" The machinery stopped. He came smiling to the front of the barge and handed the lost line to me.

From early to late, we were at this task of headering the wheat. We covered an average of forty acres per day. In the year of 1923, we cut a total of 700 acres. We were cutting farmer Heidebrecht's field of spelt wheat. It was not over a foot tall, so Father lowered the header platform so low that it barely was free of scraping the ground. Elmer and I had rest, and both of us drove barge wagon teams. Since grain was so short and we were just nipping the heads off, it was very heavy and even a medium-sized load made the horses puff to pull the heavy weight.

BOYS WILL BE BOYS

For a few days, we moved the harvesting-equipment about three or four miles North of Choteau Coulee, where the Jones and Youngs lived. We cut several days. Grandpa Neil Young had a twisted long mustache . . . his hair nicely groomed but white.

At the noon dinner table some funny things took place. Elmer and I were plagued with giggles and bursts of laughs, and Father was embarrassed with us, expecting us to be perfect angels at the table. He did not know that it was emotionally upsetting to us young boys sitting among the big men at the table.

It was evident that Grandpa Neil Young was happy and proud with his married sons at his table and a wonderful harvest being gathered. Grandpa Young picked up the cream pitcher; but Elmer and I already knew that the ladies had put horse radish in that particular cream pitcher.

Grandpa took for granted that cream was its contents, so he started to pour it into his coffee. The horse radish was thick, and it didn't come out, so he bent and tipped his head low with his exquisite twisted mustache about to wipe his plate. Having inspected the cream pitcher, he awaked that its contents were horseradish, placing it back on the table abruptly while saying: "What's horseradish doing in here?"

Elmer and I exploding with burst of laughs ... Father demanded of us, "Boys, boys, be quiet." Although Elmer and I were in a man's world, we couldn't help but still be silly boys.

MILKING IS A MAN'S JOB

Father always gave us young boys jobs that were really meant for men. Brother Elmer drove the Model T at age eight, looking through the steering wheel spokes. I remember unloading straw when very young, so why should Father make me wait to milk a cow?

In the summer of 1921, Mother said, just a few days and you will have your eighth birthday on July first. Then you may start milking cows. Now I was born in South Dakota ... five o'clock in the morning, so I was told. It may be amazing that my patience could be stretched until the evening chores. I hurried my supper meal and sneaked off to the milk house for a milk pail and a one-legged stool. I found the white-headed Bessie in the milking area.

Those cows had distinguished character names: Fanny, Short Tail, Long Horn, Crooked Horn, Molly, Rose Blackie, Whitehead, Mullah, Roan Spotie, and Bessie. I placed the stool and myself on the left side of her instead of the right side. I started to milk, and the old cow tried to tell me, "not so, you're not a sucking calf; cows are milked from the other side." So she lifts her big foot and politely walks away, leaving me sit there in the open like a dummy.

ESTHER KLASSEN'S SAD FUNERAL

The George Klassen family lived several miles west of our Montana farm. Their daughter's name was Esther, and she was a lovely young lady of twenty. One day Esther was disking farmland with a four-horse team when something provoked her horses into that stampede. Esther fell from the seat and her body was dragged and her face and skull deeply cut. Despite it all, she still possessed a beautiful countenance in her restful casket. The Lord blesses her memory.

CATS AND GOPHERS

At a time when we had too many barn cats, a certain tomcat killed a litter of infant baby kittens, and it aggravated Elmer. We dug a cat grave and found the tomcat. Elmer knocked the wind out of the cat, but apparently did not kill him. When we placed the cat in his special grave and began to shovel a heap of dirt on him, he revived and jumped out of that pool of dirt and escaped.

Brother Elmer had a baby flickertail gopher in a matchbox for a pet, but it did not last long as we could not get it to drink milk.

WASP ATTENTION

The Sunday School teacher, Mr. Klassen, did not see the wasp that made it in the building, but he did see me acting up, or so he thought I was phobia-stricken and tried to kill the mad wasp that was bothering me. The wasp stung my tender hand; it did hurt.

The teacher remarked in German, "*Das ist diena strafe.*" (That's your punishment.)

I continued to attempt to listen to the lessen with crocodile tears streaming down my face while my teacher had no mercy on me.

TROUBLED WATERS I

A late afternoon cloud burst poured water into the Choteau Coulee. Immediately after this rain, Elmer and I gathered the cattle from the north of the Coulee. Coming down the sloping hills, the waters were gathering by the moment and began to rise higher and higher. The cattle, being used to hills and water streams, had no trouble to make their way across to this point.

Elmer succeeded to back ride a cow across the swollen stream, but I had trouble catching a ride. Finally it came down to the last half-grown heifer, which feared the waters almost as much as I did. Finally she stepped down the low cliff, giving me the perfect opportunity to leap on her back. She made it across the deeper part of the waters that were over both of our heads, but she hurried through and crawled out, giving me a safe landing on the other side.

TROUBLED WATERS II

The next day, Elmer, Arthur, and I went to view the high waters that had taken out several the bridges of many roads. What a landscape with water overflowing into hundreds of feet on either side into the low plateaus, water by the acres, puffed drowned gophers and everything imaginable floating downstream.

Elmer became intrigued with some baby ducklings that floated along beside their mother ducks. Elmer's hands were full of baby ducklings, so he gave them to younger brother Arthur and told him to hold those while he caught more. I joined in the fun and we were void of fear and no sense where the drop off was into deeper waters. I saw Elmer fall in and hurried toward him to help him and fell in likewise. Fortunately the cliff made a turn right there, and we struck bottom and were able to free ourselves by crawling out. It was as though a hand of providence was guided by someone's secret prayer.

A COYOTE COMES TO SCHOOL

I believe it was in the summer of 1922 that lightening ignited a fire that burned our local schoolhouse. Other community schools were out of our township and were overloaded so the Becker family was thrown back and forth into four different schools. Near the school I was attending, some coyote hunters used hound dogs to help chase down coyotes.

When the battle was raging, and the first hounds were out of breath, they would open the second gate to let the stronger hounds take over for the death chase. A coyote must have been aware that it was life or death, and it made a turn into the school yard almost coming into the school at an open door. At the last moment, the coyote observed a coal shed with an undercrawl space, and it dived into the crawlspace under the coal shed. When the hunters caught up, they took some boards loose and pushed some of the hounds into crawlspace where they grabbed the coyote and chewed its throat right before our eyes. We all had our fill, and no one was ready to go back to class work, nor was the teacher in any mood to start teaching.

Indeed an unforgettable event.

THREE-MINUTE VEAL DRESSING

The calves that ran with the ranch cows put on weight very rapidly. As soon as they weighed 200 pounds, they were dressed out for veal. Father had prepared an apparatus, a tripod made of three long poles fastened with a rod at the top, holding block wire stretcher ropes fastened to a single tree for the leg hooks. He then would shoot a veal at a distance, bleed it, set up the tripod, and hoist the veal to clean it and then land it on his car trailer. It took three minutes to dress one veal. Usually he would load two veal and take them to the Chinook Hotels for a nice sum of money.

A SHORTHORN BULL WHO COULD NOT BE CONTAINED

About 1922, Father purchased a young bull that was enormous in size. In the stall, he would extend eight feet long. None of the neighbors' farm fences were too high for him. And he romanced about adventurously wherever he wished. Father brought home a copper bull ring and, after a very tough time drilling a channel hole, was able to install it in his nose. Father put a wire-stopper on his neck and a lengthy chain on his nose ring but all to no avail as he still went wherever he wished. Faithful Shep would rip his haunches in a mad chase, while the bull's nose chain danced from side to side. He finally wore his brute nose until it split horizontally.

Transition Back to South Dakota

Returning to South Dakota at age ten, beholding the close farm buildings, with many groves of trees, cooped me in, and I felt as if I was in cage. Twice I remember telling my uncles in South Dakota that I was homesick for Montana.

A DECISION TO MOVE BACK TO SOUTH DAKOTA

Many things led up to the decision to return to South Dakota. Repeated crop failures caused by drought, grasshoppers, gophers, and hail were probably part of the cause. Discouraged farmers did not tend to their chimneys properly, and several houses burned from this neglect. Lightning strikes had burned other homes and buildings, and even our local school went up in flames.

Homesteaders became unnerved, and I remember one couple that stopped by our farm and related that: "Yesterday, his bowels moved seventeen times."

Over a period of time, some 200 families moved from our homestead area in Montana.

Father had his moving brakes on a long time, and I remember friends at church who candidly shared the opinion that the children needed schooling but Father and Mother remained of the opinion that: "True, however, they need to learn to work also."

Elmer and I were working alongside adults, harvesting, and doing other adult work activities. It even became a joyous experience, and in some ways it was great to be an adult before you grew up.

MOTHER AND FATHER'S SOUTH DAKOTA VISIT (CHILDREN STAY IN MONTANA)

The decision for Mother and Father to visit South Dakota was a difficult thing for me to understand, and it was probably not discussed directly with the younger children beforehand. I remember waking up to the fact that Mother and Father were not there, and Chris Schmeichel, a young bachelor, was staying with us and apparently had been hired to do the chores and handle family responsibilities. Mother and Father had taken Harry, who was only six months old, and were on the Great Northern Railroad at high speed to Dolton, South Dakota, where both their parents had homesteaded in 1874.

My older sister, Bertha, was now fourteen and oversaw preparing meals for the other seven children who stayed on the farm in Montana. Lewis was the youngest left behind, and he was only two.

In South Dakota Father found that farms for rent were very hard to find. What all transpired I do not know; but Mother and Father were gone an entire month, including Christmas and the New Year.

SCARLET FEVER

When Mother and Father returned to Montana, they found that I was very sick with scarlet fever and had nearly died and I was unable to speak. Usually Mother was my nurse, but now Father played doctor. He took a little saucer, set it on top the coal stove, and poured anti-pain oil into it. That was the only medical supplies we had other than some salves. Father then rubbed that hot stuff unto my throat, asking, "How's that feel?"

In a weak voice, I was able to answer "*Gute*" (good in German).

Father was all smiles from ear to ear. No other doctor could have brought my voice back so soon.

Preparing to Move

THREE-FAMILY-FARM-SALE

Our farm machinery was sold at a three-family farm sale that was held at one of the Wall farms nearby. Homesteaders were all talking about moving, and there were very few left to do the buying. The Avery tractor was still in good shape, and it was sold with the plow. Together on the sale, the price tag could not be raised higher than eighty dollars even though the combined cost new was several thousand dollars. We sold all the larger farm implements, including two grain drills with swivel trucks, a binder, one header, two barge trailers, Bill, and Daog.

All together, the sale of farm implements did not bring enough money to pay the freight bill needed to ship what we planned to move back to South Dakota. Everything we took with us filled two freight cars, and the shipping cost was $700 which Grandmother Becker had to loan us. This debt was later repaid by deducting Father's share of her estate when Grandmother passed away in 1930.

ELMER AND FATHER JOURNEY WITH FREIGHT TO SOUTH DAKOTA

The Becker Ranch was twenty miles from Chinook, and it must have been very difficult to move so much, so far, in late winter. Elmer was twelve, and he rode Dick to drive the cattle to Chinook. How everything was loaded into those box cars during a Montana winter was a miracle. It was hard moving after a cold winter, and the cows arrived in South Dakota, looking very skinny. Our horse teams, Dick and Jim, Daisy and Dolly, George and Duey, all weathered the trip well.

Shep also survived the ordeal, and I wonder what he thought about that thousand-mile cold journey. If he could have talked, I think he would have answered, "Not as bad as that martyr clubbing I received for killing those thirty Plymouth Rock chickens."

MOTHER AND FAMILY MOVE A WEEK LATER

I still marvel at how Mother was able to handle this colossal moving affair, when concern and responsibility ate away her energy. She had so many items needing her attention all at the same time, and so many young children.

Father had asked Rev. Henry Unruh to take the rest of the family to the train depot. Rev. Unruh had used a buggy wagon, and there were both small and large trunks loaded with bedding, dishes, and clothes.

Arriving at the depot, I spotted a scale, so I immediately got on to weigh myself. I weighed seventy-seven pounds and weighed Arthur: forty-four pounds.

The depot seats were single seats with brass dividers. I stuck my feet through one side, and head at the other side, and I believe that I slept awhile.

Back row: Family: Elmer 12½, Harry 9 months, Father 40, Mother 36, Bertha 14; middle row: Ida 7, Arthur 9, Abeke 10½, Olga 5½; front row: Walter 3½, Lewis 2

On the Flier, the next day I was wide awake. A man befriended me and shared little boxes of raisins with me. They were so delicious, and the sweet taste was enjoyed repeatedly in my mind as we traveled to South Dakota.

I remember a traveler asking the conductor, "Where am I eating supper?"

The conductor answered, "Montana."

"Where did I eat dinner?"

"Montana."

"Sir, then where did I eat breakfast?"

The conductor answered, "Montana."

MEASLES OUTBREAK ON THE TRAIN

Mother faced yet another crisis on the train back to South Dakota. There was no escaping the reality of the situation, her baby, Harry, had a very high fever was breaking out with a bad case of measles while boarding the Great Northern Flyer.

In Milwaukee, we made a special transfer to another train. I think this was done in consideration of the sick child; and upon arriving, Mother received instructions that her train was waiting for her to board before leaving. I still feel the hustle-bustle between train stations.

We loaded a big-wagon carriage, which was drawn by a huge single horse driven as fast as it could go. We loaded quickly and then a whistle blew and, with shrieks and squeals of the railroad, we thundered off to Dolton, South Dakota.

ARRIVING IN SOUTH DAKOTA

We were now way ahead of schedule because of the special transfer. Mother Becker and family were not expected until late forenoon the next day, so when we arrived, there was no Father waiting. A stranger with a big car was at the depot, who observed our predicament. I believe that he spoke first, asking Mother if she needed help. A few words, and we were off to Uncle Toby Beckers. This strange man, of course, did not know where Mr. Toby Becker lived, but Mother was able to recognize enough of the community by the light of the moon, and was able to direct that strange driver exactly to Uncle Toby's Farm.

How Uncle Toby and Aunt Susie improvised enough bedding, I do not know; but in a few hours, the sun was shining, and it was breakfast time. I spoke up and said, "Mom isn't it strange, that here in South Dakota, the sun rises in the North?"

A great laugh . . . and I felt like a dummy.

Mother seeing through the predicament; cautiously spoke up, "Abeke, you are direction twisted." Pointing and saying, "North is that way."

I am still direction lost in that part of Dolton Community.

Five of the Becker children are pictured. Back row: Art, Abe, Elmer; front row: Lewis, Walter, Olga and Ida, about one year after returning to South Dakota.

DEJECTED FATHER

Father appeared so emaciated. He had been through the mill. Goodbye to the Becker reservoir, eight quarters of land, two farms, so many goodies. He just moved in the cold of winter with enough stuff to fill two freight cars at twenty miles to the depot. He was broke with an empty wallet in his rear pocket, his muscles aching and withered. He even endured some unwise remarks from his previously close friends.

ENCOURAGING UNCLE TOBY

Uncle Toby was most helpful in every way, and even brought over a big hog that was soon to deliver a litter of pigs. I became intrigued with Uncle Toby's multiple-colored rooster. In Montana, we had big Plymouth Rock hens, but this rooster was green, blue, red, and yellow, with a very stylish tail and red comb.

Uncle Toby took note, and one morning he rode over on horseback with chickens in porous sacks, including this most-beautiful bird-rooster. One day he came up missing! I wasn't aware when he disappeared, but Mother had secretly sneaked him into the frying pan.

DR. ENGBRECHT

Not long after we arrived in South Dakota, Uncle Toby's son, Delmar, not yet age three, became very sick with scarlet fever. The doctor was ten miles away in Freeman. He was a naturopathic doctor by the name of John J. Engbrecht, and he was very good with such severities.

The early spring roads were very soft and muddy. Uncle Toby picked me up on the way just in case he got stuck in the mud, to push the low range paddle on his Model T Ford, while he would push with his feet.

Several times, Delmer gave way to dying with that high fever. But with a special technique, Dr. Engbrecht helped the child revive, and he survived. Today he is a handsome young man.

Years later in 1944, I married Doctor Engbrecht's daughter, Elizabeth. See what that trip did for me.

Mother's Closing Role

I observed majestic nobility about my mother. Only a heroine could risk the twenty-mile move on the Montana plains late winter in danger of unexpected snowstorms and then make precision train-connections with eight children, including an infant coming down with measles. Her achievements stand as a testimony in the footprints of time and history.

From what I could gather, Mother had not been enthusiastic about homesteading in Montana. She loved her birthplace at Dolton, South Dakota. Her mother passed away when she was young and unmarried. Mother was an only child; and after her mother's death, her father married again. When he passed away, her stepmother remarried again. Somehow she lost her rightful inheritance that was significant, even though she was the only child. Mother wisely never communicated her losses and disappointments. It was difficult to understand Mother deeply.

I was very young when I learned some secrets about Mother. It was in connection with my "butter churn disaster." I remember getting a good spanking, which I nearly instantly turned about and showed her special love and kindness. It was heaven for both of us. Several times I remember overhearing Mother communicating my turnabouts.

In the summer of 1924, shortly after we had left Montana, we were visiting at Mother's aunt, Mrs. Jake Schmidt, for an occasion with many guests. When a bunch of the many children were to come in for the second table seating of guests. We children walked in row fashion through the porch into the kitchen and Mother's Aunt Caroline asked Mother, "And which one has those special traits?"

Mother, cautiously pointed at Abeke. This gave me a further desire to give attention to the little things that would make Mother happy.

I have never, knowingly, spoken derogatorily of my parents. In fact, I have rebuked my own brothers and sisters when they were somewhat involved in doing so.

The first spring back in South Dakota, the garden needed to be cultivated at a time when Father was sickly, so Mother hitched a team of horses and cultivated the garden. The flies were bad and irritated the horses who tramped some of the rows of beautiful garden sprouts. Mother's words were strong, and her cultivating was not a success, but shortly afterward she "prayed through" in the house.

During this same period, Bertha also was saved and baptized. In November, Bertha had complications, and then pneumonia set in. Her young life was transferred to her heavenly home on December 4, 1924, a few days before her fifteenth birthday. Bertha's cooking ability and household help, such as ironing boys' shirts, had been such a help to Mother.

Mother now found herself in deep sorrow and grief.

Mother was not much given to singing, but while we boys and Father were in the barn, doing chores, Mother burst forth, singing with deep inspiration. When we boys came to the house with Father, Mother testified that while she had been singing with all her heart that Bertha and the angels had sang with her, while she stood by the windows.

DR. MOTHER

Motherhood is precious, and all mothers are important! I would be remiss if I did not magnify the God-given healing instincts of my mother. I mentioned earlier, Elmer's fly poison, my washing machine hand scald, and I could mention others.

In March of 1926, we had just recently moved to the South Wait Ranch in Sully County, I stayed out of school, doing spring disking because Father was sickly. I was too thinly clad, and a cold northwest wind nearly froze me to the bone. I soon turned sick with double-lung pleurisy and maybe pneumonia. We had no phone, and the nearest doctor was sixteen miles away. My breathing was with short, quick pantings, my voice nearly a whisper. Mother hurried to the chicken barn and then cooked the best chicken broth to kick off the inflammation fever, and it worked!

In May, I ran barefoot and stepped on a sizable rusty nail entering deeply into my heel. Before long, my foot and ankle swelled up like a ball as poisoning set in. Mother took an apple box and made a "hood-tent" with a pan of boiling water to which she poured turpentine, while my ankle hovered over it. The boiling turpentine vapor did the trick and drew out the infection.

Dr. Mother's next patient happened to be Father. He had just left the kitchen, with a handful of matches for his blacksmith forge. Just as he entered his blacksmith shop, lightening hit and the thunder roared, making Father jerk his hand, which ignited all those matches in his hands. Gas cans were nearby, and Father could not drop the fire in his hand, so he ran outside before doing so. The sulfur fire burned his hand badly. Mother quickly ground potatoes and created potato plaster for his hand. The plaster turned green as it sucked out the sulfur and Father's hand healed quickly.

ABEKE'S BAPTISM

Mother had a big role in the character-building of her children. Just when you were at your lowest hour or point, she knew how to keep you from zeroing out. I went through such a valley in the first part of August 1933. In a great struggle, I had gotten saved and gave testimony for a public baptismal service on Sunday night, August 20th, the ordinance of Baptism to be observed the next Sunday. The Sunday School superintendent had given me a brochure on the Holy Spirit baptism. There was nothing in the brochure about water baptism, and it mentioned speaking in tongues after you receive the Spirit Baptism. The Mennonites do not practice speaking in tongues and the tract was improper for me, leaving me confused.

After a brief talk with Mother about it, she was able to give me better advice than a dozen preachers. She found herself in deep thought. Her mind most likely went back to the moment at my birth when she and Father had made a dedication for Abeke to be set aside for the ministry. She pointed out that water baptism is the church's acceptance and approval of the family of God, but that God also had a Spirit of Baptism. She stressed, *especially for preachers*, therefore not to be afraid of the anointing of the Holy Ghost. Let me put her thoughts into words: "Abeke, you're leaving the home base. Don't muff the ball. Make a home run!"

Later Father also had a talk with me, testifying that with his conversion, he also had a call to the ministry, but that it had not materialized with farming, family, moving, and only a second-grade education. He shared that naming me Abraham was to be a partaker of a heavenly calling. That week, I was cutting hay for Gottliep Mueller, and I got off the grass mower many times for prayer. I wonder if the Muellers noticed my peculiar stoppings. I was deeply impressed that both Father and Mother had intuitively spoken the exact words that my soul craved to know.

The Montana sojourn has a great impact on many lives. Heaven alone will be able to reveal the answering of prayers of our forebears and the impact of peculiar events and God's providence in many events.

Mother was hospitalized in Pierre South, Dakota, in 1933, the same year we experienced total crop failure, and a lightning strike killed fourteen cows.

MOTHER'S HOSPITALITY

Mother's policy was: If I have bread, butter and potatoes, I am not ashamed to invite anybody. Our poverty was great, and we had suffered great losses, but my mother invited a land agent, who was an acquaintance of Father, over for night lodging. His name was Mr. Joe Hofer, and he was from Bridgewater, South Dakota.

The next morning at breakfast and devotions, Father spoke up and said, "Mr. Hofer, your trip back is not far from Freeman and Sunnyside Bible School. My son Abraham and I have been talking about Bible schools. Would you be able to take him there?"

He was willing to take me, if I could get ready quickly. Mother quickly packed some shirts in an instrument case, as no suitcase was available. She packed me a pair of new striped overalls and suit. Mother put a fifty-cent piece in my hand and gave me her blessing.

Thus I was on my way, preparing for the ministry. Also continuing and struggling for six years at Sunnyside, learning also to live without money.

SUNNYSIDE BIBLE SCHOOL: ALARM CLOCK AND WARM COAT

In the fall of my first year at Sunnyside Bible School as it started getting cold, I realized that I really had a need for an alarm clock and a warm jacket, but I no money, so I just prayed. Coincidently Father and Mother just purchased an alarm clock for themselves when, lo and behold, they won an alarm clock at the grocery store. They were delighted to be able to send one of the alarms to their son at school, so they wrapped it in a blanket-lined jacket and sent it to me. How that alarm did preach to me, awakening me for the early prayer hour, and reminded me that we have a great God, who is mindful of all our little needs.

Sunnyside Bible School, May 18, 1934. Abraham Becker is the last person top row on right. Dr. John J. Engbrecht center first row. Elizabeth Engbrecht next to the right of Dr. Engbrecht.

My parents had started me off to Bible school. And all too soon, the second year found me back to school as a memorial of good will and faith, my sisters Ida and Olga receiving letters so sweet and sometimes with a token. Worn-out letters, when I glance at them: "Praying for every Day, that God shall help you and Bless you." The last stamped envelope came from Blunt South Dakota September 24, 1934 . . . just two weeks before Mother's departure.

MOTHER'S PASSING

Mother was sick with both gallstones and heart trouble and passed away twenty minutes after midnight, October 8, 1934. Funeral arrangements were in process, and I said to Father, "Mother's parents and your parents are both buried at Dolton, at the Schartner (Mennonite) Cemetery. Mother must be buried there."

Father opened his eyes widely, "Abraham, do you think it is possible to arrange a funeral so far away, a 200 miles distance?"

Blunt So Dak
April 6 - 1934

My Dear beloved Children Abe and Ida
both of you, I will write a few lines to you
to. Olga had writen a letter to you
I wish you Gods blessing, and God be with you
in all tryls and temptaion, stronghen you in him
more all the time
 My Dear beloved one, I wonted to write you
next time when I could send a few pair of sacks
to Abe, but thay havent come yet I sent for it, so
I thought its better to write a few lines this time to

let you know I love you, I pray for you
to day is a nice day Sun is shining nicly, we
washd yesterday but the wash didnt dry very good
and beside we couldt not hang every thing out side
it was windy but not very much of Sun shining, we
have to hang some outside to day
Arthur is working on the road Gravel Pit, and
have to work a few day more, Elmer is at Josh
Hoffers place Old Mr. Jacob Entz is sick
again, thay had Doktor Hart outh 4 times, and Doktor Sious
3 times,; I think I have to close now and write
next time again, Dad wont to send Abe $3.00 to
get some sunday Shoes but he had 2 Paper Bills
and one Silver Dollor so we might send next

> week the mony to Abe for Shoes
> I was thinking Ida what kind dresses you had
> for Easter, could you buy a new one, are did
> you pull through with the old ones, did you
> make eny jumper from that goods you tooke
> along from home, what else you need Abe, I'll
> send some socks as soon as I come to town
> Please write both of you, if you need somting very
> bed, , we wished very much you could of
> come here Easter vacatoon,, well you might can
> come latter on some time
>
> You ask Abe how I am feeling and Dad
> I am feeling pretty good, and Dad is pretty fair
> He said I shall write Helo to you both of you
> next month I will try to get my theeth redy
> for my mought
> well I gess this well be all for this time
> From mother

Helena Becker's letter to children Ida and Abraham, written six months before her death in October of 1934.

I said, "Let's try."

We improvised a four-wheel trailer through our friend, Mr. Robert Minder, who had a good hitch on his Model A. It was in the middle of the Great Depression, and we were only able to purchase a sixty-five-dollar casket. We had a blessed funeral. Sweet memories linger.

Helena Buller Becker's funeral (age 46 at her death). Back row: Arthur Becker, Abraham A. Becker, Elmer Becker, Ida Becker, Abraham B. Becker; front row: Harry Becker, Lewis Becker, Walter Becker, Olga Becker, Wilbert Becker

HOMEMADE TOMBSTONES

Graduating from Sunnyside Bible School in 1939, I started preaching in the summer at Des Moines and Knoxville, Iowa. It was there that I became acquainted with the Wyld Family. The Great Depression was ending, but unemployment was still rampant.

Brother Wyld thought he could produce concrete tombstones, but after making only two of them, he gave it up and said, "Abraham, you can have them."

So I was thinking of Mother's simple grave marker and picked one of them up for Mother's grave. Sometime later, I awoke up to the fact that I should have taken both of them; thus have the other one ready for Father when he passes on. Some time elapsed, and I passed through Des Moines again and picked up the other one. Then I put myself to cutting glass to fit the recessed engraving squares. Finally I finished the task, having beautifully engraved the names of Father and Mother, leaving Father's stone with the death date still open.

The day came that I wanted to show Father what I had put myself to. He was so impressed with those stones, looking at the names, birth and death dates showing up beautiful. He whimpered low cries of joy and thanks. He was most delighted. Father passed away on Oct 5, 1946. God bless his memory.

Above: Handmade tombstones

Below: Abraham B. Becker's (age 62 at death) Mother's handmade tombstone in front of the casket. Back row: David Koehn (Olga's son), Olga (Becker) Koehn, Ida (Becker) Pullman, Suzie (Glanzer) Becker (Abraham B. Becker's second wife), Harry Becker, Walter Becker, Lewis Becker, Arthur Becker, Wilbert Becker, Elmer Becker, Abe Becker, and Carol Jean Becker; front row: Julie Becker (Art's daughter), James Becker

Father's Closing Role

Cautiously and tenderly, let me speak of my father's final testimony. He was only thirteen when his father (Heinrich) Benjamin Becker, the Dakota homesteader, died. The Rev. Benjamin Becker was the first pastor of the Evangelical Mennonite Church at Dolton-Marion, South Dakota. My father and his brothers were getting quite wild for a while until a mighty revival came about, and they cleaned house, making all private and public confessions.

Father, having only a second-grade education, had yet felt a call into the ministry. Marriage and family, then the open door to the Montana open territory came first. Although he intended to play it safe with a walking plow at first, he launched out, having one goal in mind: to strike it rich. There is something worse than "bankruptcy," and that is "spiritual bankruptcy." We must learn from Luke 12:21; "So is he that layeth up treasure for himself and is not rich toward God."

Twice Father admitted the error of his ambitions, confessing the wrongs, and twice he went broke. At my birth, Father and Mother dedicated me to the ministry of the Gospel, not that I would be great or rich. Therefore, he was most delighted with my decision to become a pastor. Although I was much needed on the farm labors, he encouraged me to leave and pursue training for the ministry. He named me Abraham Jr., and I have felt a special bridge between our lives.

ANSWERS TO PRAYER

Father and Mother prayed through a few crises in their lifetime. Let me mention a few.

In the spring of 1922, Lewis was an infant of several months and suffered from severe colic pain. On Good Friday in 1922, Father and Mother fasted and spent their time praying, eating nothing the entire day. That evening, they experienced a renewal and found glorious victory in the Lord.

The winter move from the homestead in 1924 sapped Father of his vitality. The troubling trips to Dakota, sale of farming machinery in Montana for almost nothing, the challenge of loading two boxcars twenty miles away in Chinook all had taken their toll on Father. He had very little rest and few meals while journeying with the freight train over several days' duration. Followed by months of suffering, with the many new adjustments, he had a problem gaining back weight he had lost. It was prayer that found the solution. Bankruptcy and common tribulation can be our greatest asset to move us onward to Christian perfection. I praise the Lord for the unspeakable: When God can shift the ordinary to the extraordinary, the natural to the supernatural. *Hallelujah!*

Jake Koehn's house in Dakota had a grove of trees; and for a while, Father and Mother spent more time praying in the woods than they did in the house. It drew sister Bertha's attention and mine also. Bertha spent much time upstairs by the open windows, and she joined in praying with Father and Mother. While doing so, she herself prayed through to a glorious faith in Christ. Shortly afterward, she was baptized, soon before she passed away.

Father's meager education, faced with the manifold culminations, robbed him of the public church pulpit. But knowing how delighted he was with the construction of the Montana large church, having volunteered to haul the material with his Avery tractor, the many early church furnace fires, and his generous approach, kept him on target dimension.

Father's Closing Role

If not on the perfect will of God, he did his best on the good and acceptable levels of Christianity.

Mother having died in 1934, Father remarried Suzie Glanzer in 1936. They had two children together, James and Carol Jean. During these days, Father shared a heart-to-heart closeness, noting his various refillings of spiritual blessings he experienced. Father's testimony to special holiness experience late in his life has always held a sacred place in my heart. It came about through a dark season and time of struggle, and ended with a full consecration to the Lord and exuberant victory to which he more freely testified than ever before.

Near the end of Father's life, he testified so sweetly, "That he was now ready to live."

He did not say die, although he was a dying man, having had a stroke and only able to walk with a cane. My ultimate appraisal: If Father would have died rich on the golden Montana acres; he might have also died with soul poverty. Thank God for the prayers of his homesteading forebears. Father lost acres, but he died rich in grace. Father's testimonies were the last public testimonies I heard him speak. He is awaiting my arrival up yonder.

Lord help me to fulfill that quest.

Death notice for local newspaper

Abraham B. Becker

Abraham B Becker, the son of Rev. Benjamin and Susanna Becker, was born near Dolton, South Dakota, on May 13, 1884. He died Saturday, October 5, 1946. He grew up in his own community, and was married to Helena Buller in 1908, with whom he shared joy and sorrow for 28 years. To this happy union were born 11 children, two of which, Bertha, age 5, and Benjamin, an infant, preceded him in death.

In 1913 when many friends moved to Montana to homestead, this young couple also moved there, homesteaded, and farmed much ground until the year 1924, when they moved back to Dolton, South Dakota, where they lived two years. Finding the rent high and pasture scarce for cattle and horses, with which he hoped to keep his boys busy, he moved to Sully County, near Blunt, South Dakota, to once more try open range and large farming. But the Depression and much sickness brought the family back to a state of poverty.

October 8, 1934, his wife, Helena, died, which caused the family much sorrow. With the family scattering, the older children searching education and employment, Father deemed it necessary to find another companion, to which Susie Glanzer, daughter of Mr. and Mrs. Mike Glanzer, responded, and they were happily married on March 3, 1936, and were able to enjoy each other's fellowship for more than ten years. She became a real blessing to him in his seven years of sickness, when she patiently, with much toil and labor, cared for him night and day. May the Lord bless her for her faithfulness! To this union were born two children, James Edwin and Carol Jean.

In 1930 he was almost blinded in a hailstorm, when a large hailstone bruised his eye pupil. He recovered his sight doctoring with Dr. Judd of Omaha, Nebraska. Since 1939 his health failed rapidly, many times surviving miraculously. He testified to divine healing from dropsy, but he never recovered from a stroke on March 20, 1945, which left him crippled. Three weeks before his death, he lost all appetite, suffering from liver and heart trouble, during which time he prayed earnestly for his recovery and for the conversion of his children.

Father's testimony will long be remembered. He was spiritually minded, lived a devoted life, often reminding his children and testifying to them of his great conversion in his early twenties. During his prolonged sickness he prayed through to a deeper experience of holiness, and became a strict observer of giving his tithes and offerings to the cause of God. His father and mother, four brothers, and three sisters have preceded him in death.

He leaves to mourn: his wife, Susie, eight sons and three daughters, Elmer, Abraham, Arthur, Ida (Mrs. Jake Pullman, Olga (Mrs. Wesley Koehn), Walter, Louis, Harry, Wilbert, James, and Carol; two sons-in-law, five daughters-in-law, and two grandchildren, six brothers, two sisters, and a host of relatives and friends.

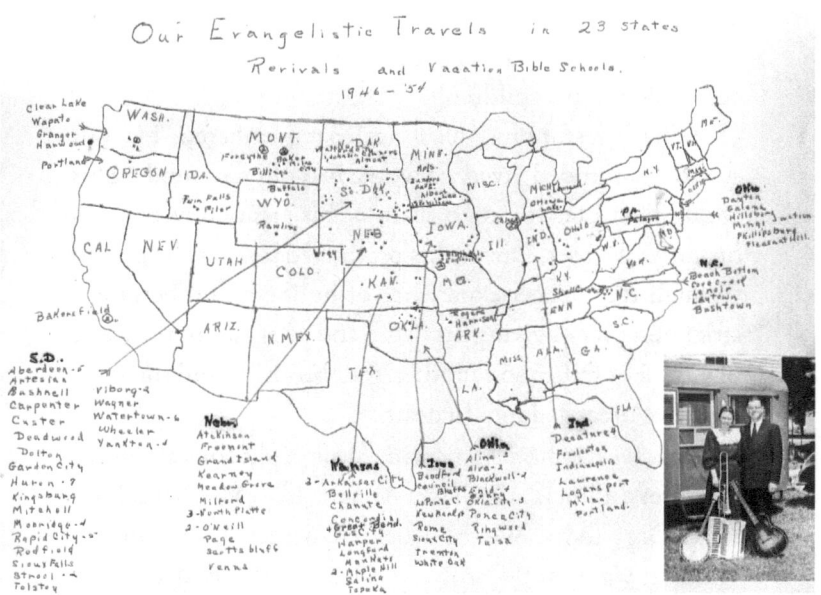

Abraham A and Elizabeth Becker's evangelism traveled to 23 states, 1946–1954

Reflecting Back

Little did my parents realize in 1933 that in a few years, I would travel with Sunnyside Bible School, as part of Gospel Tours. I spoke ninety-six times in 1937, ninety-four times in 1938, and 115 times in 1939. I also pastored churches in six different states, conducted over 175 revivals, thus preaching in twenty-six different states. I traveled the Middle East, wrote six different books on prophecy and Bible doctrine.

Thanks to the Lord God of Heaven and Earth for redeeming me, and bestowing these many by-products of Grace during my sojourn here on earth!

1982 photo: Abraham A Becker (69), Elizabeth Engbrecht Becker (69), Stephen Becker (29), Avis Mosier Becker (29), Benjamin Becker (7) and Nicole Becker (5)

Afterword

This story of Abraham and Helena's life started and ended in South Dakota, separated by a decade of adventure in Montana. Their son, my father, captured many of his Montana memories for future generations, providing a glimpse into the hardships and beauty of their lives in the early 1920s.

Their lives were undoubtedly shortened by the sacrifices made homesteading. Helena was only forty-six when she died of a stroke not long after coming back to South Dakota. She endured many heartbreaks in her forty-six years, including the death of firstborn daughter and an infant son. She was pregnant with what would have been her twelfth child when she passed, and her youngest child was only five. Abraham's children with his second wife, Susie Glanzer, were eight and four when he passed away in 1946.

Abraham and Helena's dream of a lasting legacy in Montana was not accomplished in the way they hoped. Their Montana home was not surrounded by the homes of their children and grandchildren—that dream died when they had to give up the land for back taxes and head back to South Dakota. However, they were good stewards of a legacy given to them by their forefathers—a legacy that they passed on to their descendants: FAITH that guides character development, HOPE for an eternal homeland, and LOVE that lives on.

"And now these three remain: faith, hope and love." 1 Corinthians 13:13.

Homestead foundation remnants interrupt the view of endless prairie in all directions. (2013 photo)

Hebrews 11:13 and 16, speaking about the patriarch Abraham and his wife Sarah, also fit with Abraham and Helena: "All these people were still living by faith when they died. They did not receive the things promised; they only saw them and welcomed them from a distance, admitting that they were foreigners and strangers on earth."

I met my parents' friends, Abraham and Frieda Schmidt, in South Dakota at a celebration of the church Heinrich Benjamin Becker started in the late 1800s. The Schmidts had been married close to seventy years when we enjoyed a meal together in the church basement. Soon after, Frieda sent a letter in which she wrote, "In Deuteronomy 8. Moses reminds the people to 'remember the promise made to your ancestors about this land.' We cannot act as if we do not have a heritage. None of us is self-made. We are, to one degree or another, the product of what we have been given by those who lived before us. I live in a favored land because my forbearers moved. I am relatively well to do because I inherited a work ethic and a healthy body. I am a believer because I chose to follow Christ, but my forbears made it easy for me to hear about him. We can never treasure it enough."

Amen and Amen.

—Stephen B. Becker, son of Abraham A. Becker
and grandson of Abraham B. Becker

www.ingramcontent.com/pod-product-compliance
Lightning Source LLC
Chambersburg PA
CBHW022026050526
44107CB00097B/96